LAUTRÉAMONT
AND SADE

MERIDIAN

Crossing Aesthetics

Werner Hamacher

Editor

Translated by Stuart Kendall
and Michelle Kendall

Stanford
University
Press

———

Stanford
California
2004

LAUTRÉAMONT
AND SADE

Maurice Blanchot

Stanford University Press
Stanford, California

This book has been published with the assistance of the
French Ministry of Culture—National Center for the Book.

Lautréamont and Sade was originally published in French in
1949 under the title *Lautréamont et Sade* © Les Éditions de
Minuit, 1963.

Printed and bound by CPI Group (UK) Ltd,
Croydon, CRO 4YY

Library of Congress Cataloging-in-Publication Data

Blanchot, Maurice.
[Lautréamont et Sade. English]
Lautréamont and Sade / Maurice Blanchot ; translated by
Michelle Kendall and Stuart Kendall.
p.   cm. — (Meridian : crossing aesthetics)
Includes bibliographical references.
ISBN 0-8047-4233-2 (cloth : alk. paper)
ISBN 0-8047-5035-1 (pbk. : alk. paper)
1. Lautréamont, comte de, 1846–1870.
2. Sade, marquis de, 1740–1814.
I. Title.   II. Meridian (Stanford, Calif.)
PQ2220.D723Z613 2004
841'.8—DC22
2004006881

Typeset by Tim Roberts in 10.9 /13 Adobe Garamond

Original Printing 2004

Last figure below indicates year of this printing:
13   12   11   10   09   08   07   06   05   04

Contents

Preface:
What is the Purpose of Criticism?

I cannot address many of the implications of this question. One of them deals with the senselessness of criticism itself. When we seriously contemplate literary criticism, we are under the impression that our contemplation concerns nothing serious. Journalism and the academy constitute the entirety of its reality. Criticism is a compromise between these two forms of institution. Everyday knowledge, which is prompt, capricious, fleeting, and scholarly knowledge, which is permanent and certain, unite one with the other and commingle, sometimes successfully, sometimes not. Literature remains the object of criticism, but criticism does not manifest literature. Criticism is not one of the ways in which literature asserts itself. But it is a way in which the academy and journalism are affirmed, and it derives its importance from the prominence of both of these considerable institutions, one static, the other dynamic, both of them firmly directed and organized. Naturally, we may be able to conclude from this that criticism's role is not inconsequential, since it consists in linking literature with equally important realities. This would make its role a mediating one, and the critic an honest broker. In other cases, journalism counts for less than other forms of political and ideological organization; criticism, in this case, is composed in offices, in proximity to the highest values that it must represent; the intermediary role is reduced to a minimum; the critic is a spokesperson who applies, sometimes artfully and not without a margin of freedom, general instructions. But is it not the same in every sector of life? We are talking about a mediation practiced by the critic in our Western culture: How does it work, what does it mean, what does it require? A certain level of competency, a certain facility for writing, qualities of conformity, and of good will. But this is to say little, which is not to say that it is nothing at all.

We have thus arrived at the idea that criticism is lacking in almost any substance of its own. An idea that is itself but a shadow of a larger one. Here we should immediately add that such a disparaging view as this one does not fluster criticism. It openly welcomes it, as if, on the contrary, this very lack revealed its deepest truth. When Heidegger comments on Hölderlin's poems, he says (I paraphrase): Whatever commentary might be, it will always, in regard to the poem, remain superfluous, and the last, most difficult step of interpretation is the one that leads it to become transparent before the pure affirmation of the poem.[1] Heidegger also makes use of this figure: in the noisy tumult of nonpoetic language, a poem is like a bell suspended in midair, one on which a light snow falling would be enough to make it chime, an imperceptible crashing nevertheless capable of harmoniously upsetting it to the point of discord. Perhaps commentary is just a little snowflake making the bell toll.[2]

Critical discourse has this peculiar characteristic: the more it exerts, develops, and establishes itself, the more it must obliterate itself; in the end it disintegrates. Not only does it not impose itself—attentive to not taking the place of its object of discussion—it only concludes and fulfills its purpose when it drifts into transparency. And this movement toward self-effacement is not simply done at the discretion of the servant who, after fulfilling his role and tidying up the house, disappears: it is the very meaning of its execution, which has proscribed in its realization that it eclipse itself.

All in all, the dialogue between critical and "creative" discourses is strange. Where is the unity of these two? Is it a historical unity? Is the critic there to add something to the literary work: to bring out its latent meaning (present as an absence) and to indicate its development within history, little by little raising it toward truth, where in the end the work may become stagnant? But why might the critic be necessary for this task? Why, between the reader and the work, between history and the work, should this mediocre hybrid of reading and writing insert itself, with the help of this critic who oddly specializes in reading and who, nevertheless, only knows how to read through writing, writing only about what he reads, and who must at the same time give the impression, through writing, reading, that he does nothing, nothing but let the depth of the literary work, that which resides therein, always more clearly and more obscurely, speak?

Regardless of whether one looks at criticism and the critic from a historical or literary perspective, one grasps them only through their penchant for self-effacement, through their existence always on the verge of extinction. On the side of history, insofar as history takes shape within more rigorous and also more ambitious disciplines, and is present there, not as a completed service, but as an open and fluid totality, criticism quickly relinquishes itself of itself, truly sensing that it has no right to speak in the name of history, that the so-called historical sciences and the science of historical interplay—if it existed—can and could uniquely delineate the literary work's place in history as well as its genesis within it, but might moreover pursue its indefinite advent across the widest possible range of the general movement (including the realm that the physical sciences have opened up to us). Thus the mediating role of criticism is limited to the immediate present, it belongs to the passing day and is connected to the anonymous and impersonal murmur of daily life, the understanding that runs through the streets of the world and that allows for everyone to always know everything in advance, although every individual person may still know nothing.

It might seem that criticism is a task of arduous vulgarization. Perhaps. But let us take a look at the literary side of it all, whether a novel or a poem. Consider for a moment the delicate image that we were conjuring: the snowflakes that made the bell toll. This empty movement, impalpable and a bit icy, disappears within the heated agitation it instigates. Here, critical discourse, having neither lasting effect nor reality, would like to dissolve within creative affirmation: it is never criticism that speaks, when it speaks; it is nothing. This is impressive modesty, and yet, on the other hand, perhaps not so modest. Criticism is nothing, but this nothingness is precisely that in which the literary work, silent and invisible, allows itself to be what it is: radiance and discourse, affirmation and presence, speaking seemingly about itself, without faltering, in this void of great quality that it is critical intervention's mission to produce. Critical discourse is this space of resonance within which the unspoken, indefinite reality of the work is momentarily transformed and circumscribed into words. And as such, due to the fact that it claims modestly and obstinately to be nothing, criticism ceases being distinguished from the creative discourse of which it would be the necessary actualization or, metaphorically speaking, the epiphany.

Nevertheless we feel sure that the image of snow is just an image and that we have yet even further to go. If criticism is this open space into which the poem moves, if it seeks to disappear in front of this poem, so that this poem may truly appear, this is because this space and this movement toward self-effacement (which is one of the ways in which this space manifests itself) may already belong to the reality of the literary work and also be at work within it, while it takes shape, only moving outside it when it has achieved its purpose and to accomplish that purpose.

In the same way that the necessity of communicating is not a quality added to the book, with communication, at every turn of the book's creation, catalyzing the very creation process, similarly this sort of sudden distance in which the completed work reflects itself and which the critic is called upon to gauge, is only the last metamorphosis of this opening which is the literary work in its genesis, what one might call its essential noncoincidence with itself, everything that continuously makes it possible-impossible. All that criticism does then is represent and follow outside what, internally, like a shredded affirmation, like infinite anxiousness, like conflict (or even in all other forms), does not cease to be present as a living reservoir of emptiness, of space, of error, or, better yet, as literature's unique power to develop itself while remaining perpetually in default.

Herein lies, if you will, the ultimate consequence (and a singular manifestation) of this movement of self-effacement which is one of the indications of criticism's presence: through its disappearance before the literary work, criticism recovers itself again in the work as one of its essential moments. Here, we locate a process that our era has seen develop in various ways. Criticism is no longer an external judgment placing the literary work in a position of value and bestowing its opinion, after the fact, on this value. It has come to be inseparable from the internal working of the text, belonging to the moment when it becomes what it is. Criticism is the search for and the experience of this possibility. However (to avert any misunderstanding), criticism does not have the restrictive meaning that Valéry gives it when he sees it as part of the intellect: the creative work's requirement that its value only be construed within the clarity of a thoughtful mind. "Criticism," in the sense intended here, may, even now, be closer (but the similarity remains deceptive) to the Kantian meaning of the word. Kant's critical reasoning interrogates the conditions for the possibility of scientific experience, just as criticism is connected to the search for the possibility of literary experience, but this search is not only a theoretical pursuit, it is the very process constituting the literary experience, and its possibility is constituted through testing and contesting, through creation. "Search" is a word that should not be understood in an intellectual sense, but as an action taken within and in light of creative space. Hölderlin, to again use him as an example, talks about the priests of Dionysus wandering about in the sacred night.[3] The search for creative criticism is this same errant movement, this same laborious process that opens up the darkness and is the progressive thrust of mediation, but that also risks being the endless recommencement that ruins every dialectic, procuring only failure and finding therein neither its measure nor its appeasement.

I cannot take this analysis any further here. I would however like to make one last point that appears essential. We complain about criticism no longer knowing how to judge. But why? It is not criticism that lazily refuses to evaluate, it is the novel or the poem that shirks evaluation because it seeks affirmation outside every value system. And, insofar as criticism belongs more intimately to the life of the literary work, it turns what is not able to be evaluated into the experience of the work, it grasps it as the depth, and also the absence of depth, which eludes every system of value, being on the side of what is of value and challenging in advance every affirmation that would like to get its hands on it to validate it. In this sense, criticism—literature—seems to me to be associated with one of the most difficult, but important, tasks of our time, played out in a necessarily vague movement: the task of preserving and of liberating thought from the notion of value, consequently also of opening history up to what all these forms of value have already released into it and to what is taking shape as an entirely different—still unforeseeable—kind of affirmation.

§   Sade's Reason

In 1797, *La Nouvelle Justine, ou les Malheurs de la Vertu suivie de l'Histoire de Juliette, sa soeur* was published in Holland.[1] This monumental work—nearly four thousand pages long, which its author wrote in several drafts, augmenting its length ever more, almost endlessly—immediately horrified the world. If there is a Hell in libraries, it is for such a book. One can say that no other literature of any other time has seen as scandalous a book appear, that no other book so profoundly wounded the sensibilities and convictions of men. Who in this day and age would dare compete with Sade's licentiousness? Yes, it can be claimed that here we have the most scandalous work ever written. Is this not enough to warrant its close examination and our preoccupation with it? We have the opportunity to know a work that no other writer, during any other era, has ever dared to venture beyond. We have, therefore, in some way, within our grasp, and in the so very relative world of literature, a veritable absolute, and yet, incomprehensibly, have we not sought to interrogate and examine it? We do not even dream to question it, to ask it why it is so unsurpassable, to ask what is in it that makes it so excessive and eternally too much for man to take? An extraordinary negligence. But perhaps the scandal is so pure simply because of this negligence? When we take into account all the precautions history has taken to make Sade a prodigious enigma, when we contemplate his twenty-seven years

7

in prison, his confined and restricted existence, when sequestration affects not only a man's life, but his afterlife—to such an extent that cloaking his work in secrecy seems to condemn him too, even while still living, to an eternal prison—we come to wonder if the censors and the judges who claim to lock Sade up, are not actually in Sade's service, and are not fulfilling the burning desires of his libertinage, Sade, who has always longed for solitude in the depths of the earth, for the mystery of a subterranean and reclusive existence. Ten times over, Sade formulated the idea that man's greatest excesses called for secrecy and the obscurity of the abyss, the inviolable solitude of a jail cell. Now, strangely enough, it is the guardians of morality who, in condemning him to the seclusion found within prison walls, have made themselves accomplices to intense immorality. It is his mother-in-law, the puritanical Madame de Montreuil, who, by turning his very life into a prison, makes it a masterpiece of debauchery and infamy. Similarly, if after so many years *Justine et Juliette* continues to be the most scandalous of books one can read— though reading it is nearly impossible—it is because the author and the editors, with the help of universal Morality, have taken every measure to ensure that this book remains a secret, a perfectly unreadable work, as unreadable for its length, its composition, and its ruminations as for the force of its descriptions, the indecency of his savagery, which cannot but hurl it to Hell. A scandalous, virtually untouchable book that no one can render public. But the book also illustrates that there is no scandal where there is no respect, and that where the scandal is extraordinary, the respect is extreme. Who is more respected than Sade? How many of us, even today, deeply believe that just holding this accursed book in our hands for a moment or two would make Rousseau's disdainful allegation come true: that any young girl who reads even one page of this book will be lost? Such respect is certainly a treasure for a literature and a civilization. Moreover, to all his present and future editors and commentators, can we not stop ourselves from discreetly uttering this avowal: in Sade, at least, respect the scandal.

Fortunately, Sade defends himself quite well. Not only his work, but also his thought remains impenetrable—and this is despite the fact that theoretical developments abound therein, and that he repeats them with disconcerting patience, and that his reasoning is crystal clear and sufficiently logical. A taste and even a passion for systems animates him. He explains, he affirms, he proves; he returns a hundred times to the same problem (and a hundred times is an understatement), he examines it from all angles, he explores every objection, he responds to them, he even uncovers others, and responds to them in turn. And since what he is saying is generally rather simple, since his language is copious, though specific and consistent, one might think there should be nothing easier than understanding Sade's ideology which, in him, is inseparable from the passions. And yet, what is the basis of Sade's thought? What exactly has he said? Where is the order of this system, where does it begin, where does it end? Is there anything more than a shadow of a system in the approach of this thought that is so obsessed with reason? And why do so many very well coordinated principles not succeed in forming the solid whole that they should and that they in fact seem to construct? This too remains unclear. This is Sade's primary and main peculiarity: that, at every moment, his theoretical ideas release the irrational forces that are bound up with them. These forces at once animate and frustrate his ideas, doing so with such impetus that his ideas resist these forces, and then yield to them, seeking to master this impetus, which effectively they do, but only while simultaneously releasing other obscure forces, which will lead, twist, and pervert them anew. The result is that everything said is clear, but seems at the mercy of something unsaid, which a bit later is revealed and is again incorporated by the logic, but, in its turn, it obeys the movement of a still hidden force. In the end, everything is brought to light, everything comes to be said, but this everything is also again buried within the obscurity of unreflective thought and unformulatable moments.

The reader's uneasiness when faced with this thought which is only clarified by a further additional thought which, at that moment, cannot itself be clarified, is often very intense. The read-

er's uneasiness increases even more because Sade's declared princi-
ples, which we might call his basic philosophy, appear to be sim-
plicity itself. This philosophy is one of self-interest, then of com-
plete egoism. Each of us must do what pleases us, each of us has
no other law but our own pleasure. This morality is founded on
the primary fact of absolute solitude. Sade said it and repeated it
in all its forms: nature creates us alone, there is no connection
whatsoever linking one man to another. Consequently, the only
rule of conduct is that I favor all things that give me pleasure,
without consideration of the consequences that this choice might
hold for the other. Their greatest pain always counts less than my
pleasure. What does it really matter, if the price I must pay for
even my slightest joy is an outrageous assortment of hideous
crimes, since this joy delights me, it is in me, yet the effects of my
crimes do not touch me in the least, they are outside me.

These principles are clearly stated. We find them developed in a
million ways throughout twenty volumes. Sade never tires. What
he most enjoys is holding these principles up against the ideas of
his contemporaries, their theories that all men are created equal
before nature and before the law. Thus he proposes some reason-
ing along these lines: Given that all beings are equal in the eyes of
Nature, this fact allows me the right not to sacrifice myself to pre-
serve others, whose ruin is indispensable to my happiness. Or bet-
ter yet, he drafts a sort of Declaration of the Rights of Eroticism,
with this maxim as its fundamental principle, applicable as much
for women as for men: Give yourself over to all those who desire
you, take all those you desire. "What evil do I do, what crime do
I commit when, greeting a beautiful creature, I say: 'Give me the
part of your body that can satisfy me now, and if you like, pleas-
ure yourself with the part of my body that might be pleasing to
yours?" Such propositions appear irrefutable to Sade. For pages on
end he invokes the equality of individuals, the reciprocity of
rights, without perceiving that his reasoning, far from being
strengthened by these propositions, is transformed into complete
nonsense. "Never can an act of possession be exercised on a free
human being," he writes. But what conclusions does he draw from

this? Not that it is forbidden to commit a violent act against another human being and to enjoy hurting them, inflicting them with pain against their will, but rather that no one has the right to use an exclusive relationship, one of "possession," as an excuse to refuse themselves to him. The equality of beings is the right to make equal use of all beings; freedom is the power to subject each person to his own will and wishes.

In seeing similar formulations one after another, we begin to think that there is a discrepancy in Sade's thought, something missing, a madness. We sense a profoundly deranged thought, bizarrely suspended over the void. But, suddenly, logic assumes control, our objections vanish and the system gradually takes shape. Justine, who, we know, represents worldly virtue, and who is tenacious, humble, always oppressed and unhappy, yet who is never convinced of the world's wrongs, declares suddenly in a very reasonable fashion: Your principles suppose power; if my happiness consists in never taking into account the interests of others, in occasionally hurting them, will not one day arrive when the interests of others consist in hurting me; on what grounds will I be able to protest? "Is the individual who isolates himself able to struggle against all of humanity?" This, we understand, is a classic objection. The Sadean man both implicitly and explicitly responds in numerous ways that gradually lead to the heart of his universe. Yes, he says at first, my right is that of power. And, in fact, Sadean humanity is essentially composed of a small number of all-powerful men, who had the will to raise themselves above laws and place themselves outside prejudice, who feel naturally worthy because of the deviations nature created in them, and who seek satisfaction in every way possible. These extraordinary men generally belong to a privileged class: they are dukes, kings, even the pope himself is descended from nobility; they take advantage of their status, their fortune, the impunity that their situation assures them. They owe to their birth the privileges of inequality, which they are happy to perfect through implacable despotism. They are the most powerful because they are part of a powerful social class. "I call the People," says one of them, "that vile and deplorable social class that makes its living only through pain and sweat; all who breathe must join forces against this abject social class."

But there is no doubt about it, even though these Sovereigns of debauchery often consolidate within themselves and to their own advantage the full range of inequality among the classes, this is only the expression of a historical circumstance that Sade is not taking into account in his value judgments. He is fully aware that, during the historical moment of his writing, power is a social category, that it is inscribed within the organization of society as it existed before and after the revolution, but he also believes power (like solitude) to be not only a state, but a choice and a conquest: a man is powerful when he knows how to become so with his energy. In reality, his heroes are recruited from two opposite milieux: the highest and the lowest, from the most privileged class and from the most disadvantaged class, from among the world's great individuals and from the cesspool of society's dregs. Both sets of individuals find, at the point of departure, something extreme promoting them; the extreme of misery is as powerful a stimulus as the exaltation of fortune. When one is a Dubois or a Durand, one rises up against the laws of the land because one is so restrained and too far below the laws to be able to conform to them without perishing. And when one is a Saint-Fond or the Duke de Blangis, one is too far above the law to be able to submit to it without demeaning oneself. This is why, in Sade's works, the justification for crime is an expression of contradictory principles: for some, inequality is a fact of nature; certain men are necessarily slaves and victims, they have no rights, they are nothing, against them everything is permissible. Consequently, there are the crazed eulogies to tyranny, the political constitutions intended to make the revenge of the weak and the enrichment of the poor forever impossible. "Let it be clearly understood," says Verneuil, "that it is among Nature's intentions that there necessarily be a class of individuals who by their birth and inherent weakness shall remain essentially subject to the other class."—"The laws are not made for the people ... The basic precept of any wise government is to make certain that the people shall not encroach upon the authority of the masters." And Saint-Fond: "The people shall be kept in a state of slavery that will make it quite impossible for them ever to attempt to dominate the wealthy or debase their properties and possessions." Or again: "All that goes under the name of crimes of libertinage shall never be punished, save in the slave casts."

Here we are, it seems, in the presence of the most insane theory of the most absolute despotism. Nevertheless, the perspective brusquely changes. What does Dubois say? "Nature caused us all to be equals born; if fate is pleased to intervene and upset the primary scheme of things, it is up to us to correct its caprices and, through our own skill, to repair the usurpations of the strongest... So long as our good faith and patience serve only to double the weight of our chains, our crimes will be as virtues, and we would be fools indeed to abstain from them when they can lessen the yoke wherewith their cruelty bears us down." And she adds: for the poor, crime alone opens up doors in life; villainy is their compensation for injustice, just as theft is the revenge of the dispossessed. Therefore, this has been clearly delineated: equality, inequality, freedom to oppress, rebellion against the oppressor are only completely provisional arguments through which the Sadean man's right to power is affirmed, given the difference in social strata. Besides, soon the distinction made between those who need to commit crimes to live and those who take pleasure in living only when committing crimes, dissolves. Mme. Dubois becomes a baroness. Mme. Durand, the worst kind of poisoner, rises above even princesses on the social ladder, the very princesses that Juliette does not hesitate to sacrifice to her. Counts become gang leaders, crooks (as in *Faxelange*), or even innkeepers to better rob and kill simpletons. (Though most of the victims of libertinage are found in the aristocracy, since they must be of noble birth. As the Marquis de Bressac declares with marvelous contempt to the countess, his mother: "Your days are mine, and mine are sacred.")

Now, what is happening? Some men have become powerful. Some were so by birth, but they also demonstrate that they deserve this power by the way they accrue it and enjoy it. Others have become powerful after having had recourse to criminal behavior, and the sign of their success is that they use this power to acquire freedom to commit every crime. Such is the world: some have ascended to the highest ranks of society—and around them, ad infinitum, is a nameless dust, a countless number of individuals who have neither rights nor power. Look at what becomes the rule of absolute egoism. I do what pleases me, says Sade's hero, I know only my pleasure and, to guarantee that I get it, I torture and kill. You threaten me with a similar fate the day I happen to meet someone whose pleasure is found in torturing and killing me. But I have acquired this power precisely to rise above this threat. When Sade offers us answers along these lines, we feel like we are completely slipping toward a side of his thought that is held together only by the dark forces hidden within it. What is this power that fears neither chance nor law, that disdainfully exposes itself to the terrible risks of a rule thus conceived—I will hurt you as much as I like, hurt me as much as you are able—on the pretext that this rule will always turn in its favor? Now, note that for the principles to dissolve, only one exception is needed: if only once the Powerful finds misfortune in the pursuit of his pleasure alone, if just once while exerting his tyranny he becomes a victim, he will be lost, the law of pleasure will appear to be a scam, and men, instead of wanting triumph through excess will begin again to live mediocre lives fearing the least evil.

Sade knows this. "And if your luck turns sour?" Justine asks. He will therefore descend deeper into his system and show that nothing evil will ever happen to the man actively connected to evil. This is the essential theme of Sade's work: to virtue, all misfortune, to vice, the happiness of constant prosperity. Sometimes, especially in the first drafts of *Justine*, this affirmation seems like a simple, contrived thesis that the design of the story, of which the author is master, illustrates in the guise of proofs. It seems that Sade is telling tales and believing them when he places too much store in a black Providence, which will lead those who choose to do the worst to the best. But, in *La Nouvelle Justine* and in *Juliette*, everything changes. It is obvious that Sade now has this profound conviction: that the man of absolute egoism will never fall prey to misfortune, that he will even be happy to the fullest extent and he will always be so, without exception. Madness? Perhaps. But with Sade this thought is connected to forces of such violence that they end up making, as far as he is concerned, the ideas that support them irrefutable. Actually, this theoretical certainty does not easily make its transition into doctrine. Sade takes recourse in several solutions, which he tests relentlessly, but he finds none to be satisfactory. The first is purely verbal: it consists in rejecting the social contract that, according to him, is the theoretical safeguard of the weak, and for the powerful constitutes a serious theoretical threat. In effect, the Powerful one knows very well how to make use of the law to consolidate his arbitrary power. But then he is only powerful through the law, and it is the law that then, theoretically, incarnates the power. As long as anarchy and war do not reign, the Sovereign is only the sovereign, for even if the law helps him to crush the weak, it is nevertheless through an authority created in the name of the weak and substituting the false bond of a contract for the force of a single individual. "My neighbor's passions frighten me infinitely less than the injustice of the law, for my neighbor's passions are contained by mine, whilst nothing constrains, nothing checks the injustices of the law." Nothing arrests the law, because there is nothing above the law, and therefore, it is always above me. This is why, even if the law serves me, it oppresses me. This is also why, if Sade was indeed able to see himself as sharing an affinity with the Revolution, it was only insofar as the Revolution represented for some time, between the move from one set of laws to another, the possibility of a lawless regime. He expressed ideas along these lines in these peculiar remarks: "The rule of law is inferior to that of anarchy: the most obvious proof of what I assert is the fact that any government is obliged to plunge itself into anarchy whenever it aspires to remake its constitution. In order to annul its former laws, it needs to establish a revolutionary regime wherein there is no law: this regime gives birth, in the end, to new laws, though nevertheless this second state is necessarily less pure than the first one since it is derived from it."

In fact, Power accommodates itself to any regime. It denies each one authority and, in a world made unnatural by the law, it creates a haven wherein all law is silenced, a closed place wherein legal sovereignty is ignored rather than combated. In the statutes of the "Society of the Friends of Crime," there is an article which forbids all political activity. "The Society respects the government under which it lives, and if it places itself above the law, it is because one of its principles specifies that man lacks the power to make laws that go against the laws of nature, but the always internal disorder of the Society's members must never scandalize the governed or the government." And if it does happen in Sade's writings that Power carries out some political act and mixes with the revolution—as is the case with Borchamps, who consorts with the Loge du Nord to overthrow the Swedish monarchy—the motivations that inspire it have nothing to do with the will to emancipate the law. "What are the reasons that make you so hate Swedish despotism?" one of the conspirators is asked.—"Jealousy, ambition, pride, the despair of being dominated, the desire to tyrannize others myself."—"In your opinion does the happiness of the people count for something?"—"I only have my own happiness in mind."

In extreme circumstances, Power can always maintain that it has nothing to fear from the common man who is weak, and nothing to fear from the law, the legitimacy of which it does not recognize. The real problem is the relationship between Power and power. These extraordinary men, originating from either high up the social ladder or from society's dregs, necessarily come in contact with one another: their similar tastes bring them together; the fact that they are the exception, setting them apart, brings them together. But what commonality can there be between exceptions? This question obviously preoccupied Sade. As always, he proceeds from one possible solution to another, when finally, at the end of his logic, he summons through this enigma the only word that has any importance for him. When he invents a secret society, regulated by rigorous conventions that are imposed to temper excesses therein, he has the excuse of following the example of society in his day, for Sade lived in a time when the freemasonry of libertinage, and freemasonry pure and simple, gave rise, at the heart of a society in ruins, to a large number of secret societies and clandestine colleges, founded on the complicity of the passions and the mutual respect for dangerous ideas. The "Society of the Friends of Crime" is an effort along these lines. Its statutes, analyzed and studied extensively, prohibit its members from giving in to their savage passions among themselves, specifying that these passions are only able to be satisfied in two seraglios whose populations are assured by the virtuous classes. Among themselves, the members must "give in to all their fantasies and do everything," except that, Sade says, they must not give in to their passions for cruelty. We can clearly see why: it is a question of preventing at all costs the encounter, on the grounds that they would suffer evil, of those who only derive pleasure from evil. The superior libertines rally together, but do not encounter one another.

Such a compromise cannot satisfy Sade. It is also necessary to note that, although the heroes of his books constantly join forces through conventions that limit their power and superimpose order on their disorder, the possibility of betrayal remains constant: between accomplices, tension never ceases to grow, to the point that they, in the end, feel less connected by the oath of allegiance that unites them than by the reciprocal need to break this oath. This situation makes the entire last section of *Juliette* very dramatic. She has principles. She has respect for libertinage and when she encounters an accomplished villain, the perfection of the crime she attributes to him, the power of destruction that he represents, not only lead her to join forces with him, but, even when this association becomes dangerous for her, leads her to spare his life if she can. So, although in danger of being killed by the monster, Minski, she refuses to have him killed. "This man is too much of a nuisance to humanity for me to deprive the universe of him." But then there is another character who thinks up lecherous masterpieces, and yes, in the end she sacrifices him, but only because she saw that upon leaving these bloody orgies he usually went to church to confess and purify his soul. Therefore, would the perfect criminal be protected by the passions that consume him? Would there remain one last principle that stipulates that the libertine can never be the object or the victim of his own libertinage? "You have told me a hundred times," says Mme De Donis to Juliette, "that libertines do not harm each other; do you go against this maxim?" Her response is clear: she contradicts the maxim; Mme de Donis is sacrificed; and then one by one her most beloved accomplices, her most respected compatriots in debauchery perish as victims either of their fidelity, or of their perjury, or of their lassitude, or even of the fervor of their feelings. Nothing can save them, nothing exonerates them. Juliette no sooner hastens her best friend's death than she sets her sights on new allies and exchanges a vow of eternal allegiance with them—vows they themselves have mocked, since they are fully aware that they are putting limits on their excessive behavior only for the sheer enjoyment of breaking these limits.

The following conversation between a few of the masters of crime summarizes the situation quite well. One of them, Gernand, says this about his cousin Bressac: "Well, he will receive an inheritance from me; and I wager that my life doesn't irritate him: I have the same tastes, the same way of thinking; he is sure to find a friend in me." Certainly, says Bressac, I will never hurt you in the least. Meanwhile, the same Bressac notes that another of his relatives, d'Esterval, who specializes in gutting passers-by, was very close to killing him. "Yes," says d'Esterval, "but as a relative, never as a compatriot of debauchery." But Bressac remains skeptical, and everyone can't help but agree that this consideration very nearly failed to restrain Dorothy, d'Esterval's wife. Now what was Dorothy's response? "Your eulogy is in your death sentence. I have this terrible habit of sacrificing the men I am attracted to, which traces your death sentence back to my declaration of love." All this is clear. But, under these conditions, what becomes of Sade's theory of the pleasures of Evil, what becomes of this certainty that a man who has all vices will be continuously happy, while the man who has even a single virtue will necessarily be plagued by misfortune? In truth, his writings are littered with the corpses of libertines, struck down at the height of their glory. It is not uniquely Justine that misfortune pursues, but the superb Clairwill, Sade's most powerful and tireless heroine, and Saint-Fond, killed by Noirceuil, and the licentious Borghese, thrown into the pit of a volcano, and hundreds of perfect criminals. What strange denouements and unusual triumphs of these perverted men! How can Sade's deranged reasoning be blind to all the glaring contradictions it contains? Nevertheless, these contradictions are, in fact, proof and confirmation of his reasoning, and this is why:

When we read *Justine* absentmindedly, we let ourselves be taken in by a rather vulgar piece of literature. We see this young virtuous girl continuously raped, beaten, tortured, the victim of a destiny that is bound to destroy her; and when we read *Juliette*, we see a young, lecherous girl flit from pleasure to pleasure. Such a plot hardly convinces us. We have, however, not paid close enough attention to its most important aspect: being attentive only to the sadness of the former and to the satisfaction of the latter, we neglected to notice that at base both stories of the two sisters were identical, that everything that happens to Justine happens to Juliette, and that both of them endure the same experiences, overcome the same difficulties. Juliette is also thrown in prison, beaten up, promised torture, and tortured endlessly. Hers is also a horrible existence, but here is the difference: these evils give her pleasure, these tortures enthrall her. "How delicious are these implements of torture, of the crime that we love." And we are not even talking about those unusual tortures that are so terrible for Justine and so completely delightful for Juliette. In the course of one episode, which takes place in the corrupt judge's chateau, we see the unfortunate Justine subjected to truly abominable torture; her suffering is unheard-of; we can only think it a considerable injustice. Then what happens? A completely lecherous girl, who is observing the goings-on, becomes enraged by this spectacle, demands that she be made to withstand, then and there, the same torture. And she derives infinite pleasure from it. It is therefore absolutely true that virtue gives rise to man's misfortune, but not because it exposes man to unfortunate events. It is because, if one is stripped of one's virtue, what was previously misfortune becomes an opportunity for pleasure, and what was torment becomes voluptuous.

For Sade, the sovereign man is inaccessible to evil because no one can hurt him. He is the man consumed by every passion, and his passions take pleasure in everything. We occasionally accepted, as the expression of a paradox too spiritual to be true, Jean Paulhan's conclusion that, behind Sade's sadism, a completely opposite penchant appeared.[2] We see, nonetheless, that this idea is the heart of Sade's system. The man of complete egoism is a man who knows how to transform all distaste into tastes, all repugnance into attractions. Like the philosopher of the bedroom, he asserts: "I love it all, I enjoy myself with everything, I want to bring together genders, races, things, and people of all kinds." And this is why Sade, in *The 120 Days of Sodom*, sets about accomplishing the enormous task of completely enumerating every anomaly, every distraction, every human possibility.[3] He must experience everything in order to be at the mercy of nothing. "You will know nothing if you have not known everything, and, if you are timid enough to content yourself with nature, it will forever be outside your grasp."

We understand why the forlorn Justine's objection, "And if your luck should change?", cannot trouble the criminal heart. Luck can change and become bad luck, but then it will be a new and different luck, just as desired, as satisfying as the previous one. But you risk going to the scaffold! You might perhaps meet your end in one of the most ignominious of deaths!—This is indeed my most cherished desire, the libertine responds. "Oh, Juliette," says Borghese, "I would like my deviations to guide me as if I were the last of all creatures to the fate to which their abandon carries them. The gallows would be for me a throne of voluptuousness. There, I would brave death while delighting in the pleasure of expiring a victim of my horrendous crimes." And again: "The true libertine loves even the reproaches he receives for the unspeakable deeds he has done. Have we not seen some who loved the very tortures human vengeance was readying for them, who submitted to them joyfully, who beheld the scaffold as a throne of glory upon which they would be most grieved not to perish with the same courage they had displayed in the loathsome exercise of their heinous crimes? There is the man at the ultimate degree of meditated corruption." Against such a Power, what can the law do? It intends to punish such a man, but it rewards him, and it thrills him by demeaning him. And, likewise, what can the libertine do against his counterpart? One day he betrays him and sacrifices him, but this betrayal arouses intense pleasure for the one who falls victim to it, and he sees all his suspicions confirmed therein and dies in the voluptuousness of the thought of having been the excuse for a new crime (not to mention the other titillations involved). One of Sade's most curious heroines, Amélie, lives in Sweden; one day, she goes looking for Borchamps, the conspirator we mentioned earlier; the one who, in hopes of a mass execution on a monstrous scale, has just delivered all the members of the conspiracy to the reigning sovereign, the king. His betrayal has excited the young woman. "I love your ferocity," she tells him. "Promise me that one day I too will be your victim; since the age of fifteen, my mind has been obsessed with the idea of perishing the victim of the cruel passions of libertinage. Of course, I do not want to die tomorrow; my eccentricity does not go that far; but I do only want to die in this manner: becoming, while expiring, the excuse for a crime is an idea that makes my mouth water." A strange mind, truly worthy of this response: "I am crazy in love with your mind, and I think we will do amazing things together."—"She is rotten, putrefied, we are a perfect match!"

Thus, everything is beginning to crystallize: for the integral man, who is all men, no evil is possible. If he inflicts pain on others, what exquisite pleasure! If others inflict pain on him, how delightful! Virtue delights him, for it is weak and he crushes it. And vice also pleases, because he derives satisfaction from the disorder it invokes, even though it is at his expense. If he lives, there is absolutely no event or occurrence that he is unable to transform into pure happiness. If he dies, he finds an even greater happiness in death, the consciousness of his destruction becoming the coronation of a life that alone justifies the need for destruction. He is therefore inaccessible to others. No one can undermine him, nothing can take away his power of being contained within a body and enjoying himself. Such is the primary meaning of his solitude. Even if he, in turn, seemingly becomes a victim and a slave, the violence of the passions that he knows how to assuage in any circumstance assures him of his sovereignty, makes him feel that in any circumstance, in life and in death, he shall remain all-powerful. Despite the similarity of descriptions, it seems right to allow Sacher-Masoch the paternity of masochism and Sade that of sadism. For Sade's heroes, the pleasure of degradation never taints their supreme self-mastery, and abjection exalts them. All these feelings, shame, remorse, a fondness for punishment, remain foreign to them. As Saint-Fond declares to Juliette: "My pride is such that I would like those who serve me to kneel, and never to speak to them except through a spokesperson." And she responds (not ironically) with this question: "But do not the caprices of libertinage free you from this haughtiness?"—"For minds assembled like ours," answers Saint-Fond, "this humiliation caters deliciously to our pride." And Sade adds in a footnote: "This is easily understood; one does what no one does; we are therefore unlike any other." On the moral level, there is the same proud satisfaction in the feeling of being ostracized from humanity: "It is necessary for the world to tremble upon learning of the crimes we will have committed. We must force men to blush for belonging to the same species as us. I demand that a monument be built commemorating this crime to the universe and that our names be engraved on it by our own hands." A Unique Being, unique among men, this is truly a sign of sovereignty, and we will see just how far Sade wants to push this status.

Everything is now beginning to become even clearer, but at this point we also have the sense that everything is beginning to become extremely obscure. The agile move with which the Unique Being eludes the other's grasp is far from transparent. From certain angles, it can be seen as a kind of stoic imperviousness, which seems to suppose man's complete autonomy with respect to the world. Yet, at the same time, it is the exact opposite: since he is independent of others who can never harm him, the Unique Being suddenly asserts a relation of absolute domination over them. And he can do this not because others have nothing on him except a dagger, or torture, and not because their schemes for debasement leave him intact, but because he can do anything to them, so that even the pain they cause him provides him with the pleasure of power and helps him exert his sovereignty. Now, this situation is rather embarrassing. When "being the master of myself" means "being the master of others," when my independence does not come from my autonomy, but from the dependence of others on me, it is obvious that I forever remain connected to others and that I need them, even if only to obliterate them. Such a difficulty has often been evoked in regard to Sade. It is not clear that Sade is even conscious of it, and one of the innovations of this "exceptional" thought perhaps originates with this point: when one is not Sade, this is a crucial problem, through which relations of reciprocal solidarity between master and slave are reintroduced; but when one is Sade, there is no problem and it is moreover impossible to see a problem in any of this.

We are incapable of examining, to the extent that would be necessary, each of Sade's numerous texts (everything is always in abundance when it comes to Sade) that make reference to this situation. In truth, contradictions abound. On a few occasions, the fervor of the libertinage seems haunted by the contradiction of his pleasures. The libertine knows no greater pleasure than sacrificing his victims, but this pleasure is his very downfall, it self-destructs while annihilating its very cause. "The pleasure of killing a woman," says one, "is soon over; she no longer feels anything when she is dead; the pleasure of making her suffer disappears along with her life... Let's brand her (with a red hot iron), let's mark her indelibly; with this deprivation she will suffer to the last moment of her life and our lust, infinitely prolonged, will thereby become even more delicious." Similarly, Saint-Fond, dissatisfied with simple methods of torture, desires a kind of perpetual death for each being. This is why, through an incontestably ingenious system, he devises to get his hands on Hell, to have at his disposal in our world, at his victims' expense, this inexhaustible resource for methods of torment. We discern herein, assuredly, just what sort of inextricable alliance oppression created between the oppressed and the oppressor. The Sadean man draws his existence from the death that he inflicts and at times when, desiring eternal life, he dreams about a death he can continuously impose. Then, the executioner and the victim, one forever facing the other, see one another bestowed equally with the same power, with the same divine attribute of eternity. We would not know how to argue with the fact that such a contradiction is part of Sade's thought. Yet, even more often, he passes beyond all this by means of reasons that open up for us a more profound view of his world. Clairwell scolds Saint-Fond for what she calls his unforgivable eccentricities, and setting him anew on the right path she gives him this word of advice: "Get rid of that voluptuous idea that warms your loins—the idea of indefinitely prolonging the torture of the Being you intend to kill—and replace it with a greater number of murders. Do not drag out the murder of one individual, which is impossible, but kill many of them, which is very feasible." The greater number is, in fact, a more perfect solution. To consider human beings from the standpoint of quantity kills them more completely than does the physical violence that annihilates them. The criminal unites, perhaps, in an indissoluble way with the man he kills. But even while sacrificing his victim, the libertine, on the other hand, only experiences the need to sacrifice a thousand more. He seems strangely free of any connection to his victim. In his eyes, his victim does not exist for him or herself, his victim is not a distinct being, but a simple component, indefinitely exchangeable, within an enormous erotic equation. To read declarations like this one—"Nothing is more enjoyable for me, nothing excites me like a large number of beings"—we better understand why Sade makes use of the idea of equality as support for so much of his argumentation. All men are equal: this means that no creature is worth more than another, every being is interchangeable, each one has only the meaning of one unit within an infinite number. Before the Unique Being, all beings are equal in worthlessness, and the Unique Being, as he reduces them to nothing, only makes this nothingness manifest.

This is what makes Sade's world so strange. Scenes of ferocity succeed scenes of ferocity. The repetitions are endless and fabulous. In a single scene, each libertine frequently tortures and massacres four or five hundred victims; then it starts over again the next day; then, that evening, a new ceremony. The proceedings vary slightly, things get heated up again; and massacre compounds massacre. But is it not obvious that those who meet their end in these outrageous murders, those who die, already lack the slightest bit of reality, and if they disappear at the hands of this derisive facility, they were annihilated beforehand by an act of total and absolute destruction, they are there and they do die, but only to bear witness to this kind of original cataclysm, this destruction that is not only their own, but also everyone else's? This is striking: the world in which the Unique Being exists is a desert; the beings he encounters there are less than things, less than shadows. And while tormenting them and destroying them, he does not seize upon their life, but verifies their nothingness. He becomes master of their nonexistence, and he draws great pleasure from this. What then does the Duke de Blangis say, at the dawn of the 120 days, to the women gathered there for the pleasure of the four libertines? "Examine your situation, who you are, who we are, and allow these thoughts to make you tremble; you are now outside the borders of France in the heart of an uninhabited forest, beyond the steep and pointy mountains whose passageways have been obstructed immediately after you crossed them; you are shut up within an impenetrable citadel; whoever it is you think you are, you are hidden from your friends, from your family; *you are already dead to the world.*" This must be taken literally: these women are already dead, eliminated, locked up in the absolute void of a bastille where existence no longer penetrates and where their lives serve no other purpose than to manifest this quality of "already dead" with which their lives now intermingle.

We are setting aside the stories of necrophilia which, although numerous in Sade's work, seem rather far from the "normal" propensities of his heroes. Besides it would be necessary to indicate that, when his heroes exclaim "Ah, what a beautiful cadaver!" and become excited by the imperviousness of death, they have, for the most part, begun their careers as murderers, and they are, in fact, striving to extend the effects of this capacity of aggression beyond death. It is undeniable that what characterizes Sade's world is not just the fondness for becoming one with the immobilized and petrified existence of a corpse, nor is it the attempt to slip into the passivity of a form representing the absence of any form, of a completely real reality, taken from the uncertainty of life and meanwhile incarnating the ultimate unreality. On the contrary, the center of Sade's world is the necessity for sovereignty to affirm itself through an enormous negation. This negation, which is carried out on a massive scale, which no individual instance is enough to satisfy, is essentially destined to surpass the plane of human existence. Although the Sadean man uses his power to impose himself on others with the intention of destroying them, if he gives the impression of being independent of them, even when displaying the necessity to annihilate them, if he seems forever capable of doing without them, it is because he has set himself apart, on a level where he no longer has anything in common with them, and because once and for all he has placed himself on this plane to make the scope of his destructive project into something that eternally surpasses man and his puny existence. In other words, insofar as the Sadean man appears surprisingly free in relation to his victim, upon whom however his pleasure depends, it is because the violence is directed at something other than his victims, it goes truly beyond them and only assists in verifying frenetically, infinitely, with each individual case, the general act of destruction through which he reduces God and the world to nothing.

Obviously, with Sade, the spirit of crime is connected to the dream of unlimited negation that weak, practical possibilities never cease to debase and dishonor. The most magnificent crime in this world is the sort of tribulation that makes the libertine blush. There is not one among them who, like the monk Jerome,

does not feel shame at the thought of the mediocrity of his hor-
rendous crimes and seeks a superior crime to any that man might
commit in this world. "And unfortunately," he says, "I have not
found one; all that we do pales in comparison to what we would
like to be able to do." "I would like," says Clairwill, "to find a
crime whose continual effects are on-going, even when I am no
longer enacting them, so that there will never be one single
moment in my life when, even while I sleep, I am not creating
some disorder or another. And this disorder should extend to the
point of general corruption or such categorical disruption that
even after I die the effects will still reverberate." To which Juliette
gives this very proper response, pleasing to the author of *La
Nouvelle Justine*: "Try committing a moral crime, one that can
only be accomplished through writing." If in his system Sade
reduced the pleasures of the mind as much as he possibly could, if
he almost completely did away with the eroticism of the imagina-
tion (because his own erotic dream consists in projecting, onto
characters that do not dream but instead act out in reality, the
unreal movement of his pleasures: Sade's eroticism is dreamed
eroticism, since it is realized, for the most part, only in words; yet
the more this eroticism is that of a dream, the more it demands
narration from which the dream is banished, wherein debauchery
is realized and lived), if Sade has however elevated, in an excep-
tional way, the imaginary, it is because he comprehends wonder-
fully that the basis for so many imperfect crimes is an impossible
crime which the imagination alone can contemplate. And this is
why he leaves it to Belmor to say: "Oh, Juliette, how delicious are
the pleasures of the imagination! The entire earth belongs to us in
these wonderful moments; not one single creature resists us, we
devastate the world, we repopulate it with new objects which we
again sacrifice; we have the capacity for all these crimes, we enjoy
every bit of it, we multiply the horror by a hundred."

In a collection of essays that not only expresses some of the most
powerful thoughts about Sade but also about all the problems that
Sade's existence can clarify, Pierre Klossowski explains the very
complex character of the relations that the Sadean consciousness

maintains with God and his neighbor.[4] He shows that these rela-
tions are negative, but that, insofar as this negation is real, it rein-
troduces the notions that it abolishes: the notion of God and the
notion of the neighbor, Klossowski says, are indispensable to the
libertine's consciousness. We could discuss this endlessly, because
Sade's work is a chaos of clearly stated ideas in which everything is
said, though in which everything is also hidden. After all, Sade's
originality seems to be in the extremely firm assertion of founding
man's sovereignty on the transcending power of negation, a power
that depends in no way upon the objects that it destroys, which,
in order to destroy them, does not even suppose their existence
beforehand, because when it destroys them it has always previous-
ly considered them as nothing. Now, this dialectic uncovers simul-
taneously its best example and, perhaps, its justification insofar as
the Almighty Sade is affirmed with respect to the divine Almighty.

Maurice Heine has celebrated the exceptional resolution of
Sade's atheism.[5] But, as Pierre Klossowski frequently observes, this
atheism is by no means dispassionate. The moment the name of
God appears in even the most tranquil of passages, the language
suddenly begins to burn, the tone rises, the impelling force of hate
directs the words, overturns them. It is certainly not through the
scenes of lust and lechery that Sade's passion is revealed, and each
time the Unique Being perceives some vestige of God in his path,
it is then that violence, contempt, the fervor of pride, and the anx-
iety of power and desire immediately ensue. In some ways, the
idea of God is the inexpiable fault of man, his original sin, the
proof of his emptiness, what justifies and authorizes crime, for we
cannot be too forceful in our efforts to annihilate a being who is
willing to bow down and prostrate himself before God. Sade
writes: "The idea of God is the one wrong that I am not able to
forgive man." Decisive words and a key to his system. Belief in an
almighty God who allows man only the reality of a wisp of straw,
of an atom of nothingness, imposes on the complete man the obli-
gation to seize this superhuman power, and to himself exert, in the
name of man and on men, the sovereign right that these men have
recognized to be God's. When he kills, the criminal is God on

Earth, for he realizes between himself and his victim the relation-
ship of subordination wherein he sees the definition of divine sov-
ereignty. When a true libertine discerns, even in the mind of the
most corrupt debauchee, the slightest bit of religious faith, he
immediately decrees his death: for this poor immoralist has
already destroyed himself, by surrendering to the hands of God.
He considers himself to be nothing, so he who kills him is only
regulating a situation that appearances barely veil.

The Sadean man negates men, and this negation is carried out
through the intermediary of the notion of God. He momentarily
becomes God, so that, when in his presence, other men become
inconsequential and then realize exactly to what extent a being
before God is sheer nothingness. "Do you not love men, my
prince?" asks Juliette—"I deplore them. There is not one instant
wherein I am not concocting the most violent ways to harm them.
In fact, there does not exist a more pathetic race ... How base, how
vile man is, how disgusting!"—"But you," Juliette interrupts, "do
you really believe that you are one of them, that you are a man?
Oh, no, no, when you dominate them with such force, it is impos-
sible that you are one of them."—"She is right," says Saint-Fond,
"yes, we are gods."

Meanwhile, the dialectical movement perseveres: the Sadean
man assumes the power to rise above other men, this power stu-
pidly given to God by these same men. The Sadean man does not
forget for one moment that this power is entirely negative. Being
God can only mean one thing: crushing men, annihilating cre-
ation. "I should like to be Pandora's box," Saint-Fond says, "so
that all the evil released from my heart destroys each and every
being individually." And Verneuil says this: "If it was true that a
God existed, would we not all be his rivals destroying as we do
what he has molded?" This is how an ambiguous conception of
the Almighty is gradually conceived, though there can hardly
therefore be any doubt about its implications. Klossowski empha-
sizes the theories of Saint-Fond, whose views we have just inti-
mated and who, among all of Sade's heroes, presents the singular
trait of believing in the Supreme Being; only this God in whom

he believes is not very good, but "very vindictive, very barbaric, very mean, very unfair, and very cruel"; it is the Supreme Being of meanness, the God of evil acts. Sade has drawn all kinds of brilliant developments from this idea. He imagines a Last Judgment which he describes with all the resources of the ferocious humor he possesses. We hear God berate these fine men with the following words: "When you have seen that everything on earth is vicious and criminal, why did you stray onto paths of virtue? Has the perpetual misery in which I cloak the universe not been enough to convince you that I love only disorder and that you have to annoy me to make me happy? Did I not every day furnish you with examples of destruction? Why are you not destructive? Imbecile! Can't you just imitate me!"

But having brought this to the fore, it is obvious that this conception of an infernal God is only a moment in the dialectic wherein Sade's superman, after repudiating man in the name of God, finally meets God and then, in turn, rejects him in the name of Nature, only to, in the end, renounce Nature, equating it with the spirit of negation. In the evil God, the negation, after having just exterminated the notion of man, takes a short breather, so to speak, before turning its attention inward, on itself. In becoming God, Saint-Fond simultaneously makes God become Saint-Fond. And the Supreme Being, into whose hands the weak have delivered themselves as examples to compel the strong to abdicate themselves as well, no longer reaffirms Himself except as the gigantic pressure of a bronze-like transcendence which crushes each being in proportion to his weakness. This is the hatred of man hypostatized, raised to its highest degree. Yet, having just attained absolute existence, the spirit of negation, having as such become conscious of itself as infinite, now has no other choice than to turn against the affirmation of this absolute existence, perhaps now the only object on the same level as infinite negation. This hatred of men was embodied by God. Now this hatred of God liberates hate from God. Such aggressive hate seems at every moment to be projecting the reality of what it denies, to better affirm and justify itself. "If this existence—God's existence—were proven true, I must admit," says Dubois, "the sheer pleasure of perpetually irritating such a being would necessarily become the most precious compensation for the fact that I would find myself believing in him." But does such a scalding hate affirm, as Klossowski seems to believe, a faith that had forgotten its name and resorted to blasphemy in order to force God to end his silence? We are not fully convinced that this is the case. Everything indicates the contrary, that the only reason behind his predilection for the fierce hatred of God was that in Him he found a privileged pretext and aliment. For Sade, God is obviously only the mainstay of his hatred. His hatred is too great to be contained by just one object; since it is infinite, since it always goes beyond every limit, it takes pleasure in itself and becomes ecstatic in this infinitude to which it gives the name God ("Your system," Clairwill says to Saint-Fond, "is based only on the deep horror that you have for God."). But this hatred alone is real and, in the end, it will focus its attention on Nature with as much boldness as it displayed against the nonexistent God it abhors.

Indeed, if all things religious, if the very name of God, if priest-like these "God-makers" excite Sade's most tempestuous passions, it is because the words of God and religion embody nearly every form of his hate. In God, he hates the nothingness of man—who created such a master for himself—and the thought of this nothingness so irritates and enrages him that he is left no other choice than to work with God to sanction this nothingness. He furthermore hates God's omnipotence, in which he sees what is rightfully his own, and God becomes the face, the body of his infinite hatred. Finally, in God he hates the misery and misfortune of God, the pointlessness of an existence that, for as much as it affirms itself as existence and creation, is nothing. For what is great, what is everything, is the spirit of destruction.

This spirit of destruction, in Sade's system, is identified with Nature. With this point Sade grappled and groped, and in fact he had to renounce the then-popular atheist philosophies, for which he particularly felt an affinity and wherein his reasoning, thirsty for arguments, found inexhaustible resources. But insofar as he was able to go beyond naturalist ideology, and insofar as he never fell prey to outside analogies, he proves that in him logic was brought to its end without giving way to the dark forces and ominous figures that supported it. Nature is one of the words that he writes, like so many writers of his time, the most willfully. It is in the name of Nature that he leads the struggle against God and against all that God represents, morality in particular. We find no need to push this point any further, given that the amount Sade himself wrote on this subject is vertiginous. Nature is firstly, for him, universal life and, for hundreds of pages, his entire philosophy consists in repeating over and over that only immoral instincts are good, since they are facts of Nature, and the first and final authority is that of Nature. In other words, that there is no morality is the reigning fact. But then, irritated by the equal value that he feels obligated to accord virtuous instincts and evil impulses, he attempts to establish a new hierarchy of values with crime at the summit. His principal argument states that crime is more on the side of Nature, because it is movement or, in other words, it is life; Nature, which thrives on creation, he says, needs crime, which destroys. All this is established in a very detailed way, at endless length and sometimes with rather striking proofs. However, by continually talking about Nature, finding himself constantly confronted with this insurmountable and sovereign presence, the Sadean man gradually becomes aggravated. This irritation fuels his anger and crystallizes his feelings for Nature into intense hatred. Nature, now completely unbearable to him, becomes the focus of his anathemas and negations. "Yes, my friend, yes, I abhor Nature." This insubordination has two deep-seated motivations. On the one hand, he finds it intolerable that the power of incredible destruction, which he represents, has no other purpose than to authorize Nature to create. On the other hand, insofar as he is himself part of Nature, he senses Nature evade his negation, and the more he outrages Nature and the more he serves it, the more he annihilates it and the more he submits to its law. From then on, hate-filled screams, a truly mad rebellion. "O you, blind and mindless force, when I have exterminated all the creatures that cover the earth, I will still be truly far from my goal, since I would have served you, cruel mother, and since I only aspire to avenge myself of your negligence and meanness which you inflict on men, while furnishing them with the means to free themselves from the frightful penchants that you inspire in them." With this, we see the expression of a primordial and elemental sentiment: to outrage nature is man's deepest necessity; this need is, in him, a thousand times stronger than the one he has to irritate God. "In all that we do, there are only offended idols and creatures, but Nature is not one of them, and Nature is the one I really want to outrage; I would like to upset its plans, to foil its proceedings, to stop the orbit of the stars, to disrupt the planets that float in space, to destroy all that serves it, to protect all that harms it, in a word, to insult the core of Nature; and I am incapable of this." And yet, in this passage, Sade takes the liberty of intermingling Nature with its great laws, which allows him to dream of a cataclysm that could destroy these very laws. But his logic rejects this compromise and when, elsewhere, he imagines an engineer inventing a machine to pulverize the universe, he must confess that nobody else is more deserving of nature than him. Sade is fully aware that annihilating all things is not the same thing as annihilating the world, because the world is not only a universal affirmation, but universal destruction as well. In other words, the entirety of being and the entirety of nothingness reveal it equally. This is why man's struggle with nature is engendered, within the history of man, at a dialectical stage truly superior to that of his struggle with God. We might say, without modernizing his thought, that Sade is one of the first to have seen in the idea of the world the very markings of transcendence, since, with the idea of nothingness being part of the world, we can only consider the nothingness of the world within a totality which is always the world.

If crime is the spirit of Nature, there can be no crime against nature, and, consequently, no crime is possible. Sade asserts this, sometimes with great satisfaction, sometimes with fiery rage. Denying the possibility of crime allows him to deny morality, God, and all human values, but the denial of crime also entails relinquishing the spirit of negation, admitting that this spirit could itself be usurped. He vigorously opposes this conclusion, which leads him gradually to remove all reality from Nature. In the last volumes of *La Nouvelle Justine* (most notably in Volumes VIII and IX), Juliette renounces all of her previous conceptions and makes amends in the following way: "What an imbecile I was, before we parted ways I was still part of Nature, but the new systems I've adopted since then have relieved me of Nature... " Nature, she says, has no more truth, reality, or meaning than God himself: "Ah! Bitch, you are perhaps deceiving me, since I was deceived so in the past, with the infamous deified chimera to which, we were told, you were subjected; we are not depending on you any more than on him; the causes have perhaps no relation to the effects... " Thus Nature disappears, although the philosopher placed much store in it and although Sade found the idea of making a formidable machine of death out of universal life very agreeable. Yet nothingness alone is not his goal. What he has pursued by pushing the spirit of negation to its limit is sovereignty. So that this negation would be felt in the most extensive way, he used alternately men, God, and Nature. Men, God, and Nature: When negation crosses with each of these notions, it appears to bestow on them a certain kind of value, but if we take this experiment into account in its entirety these moments no longer have the least bit of reality, because the peculiarity of the experiment consists specifically in obliterating these moments, annihilating one after another. What exactly are men, if they are the vast nothingness before God? What is God, in the presence of Nature? What is Nature, which is forced to disappear by man's need to outrage it? And so the circle closes. Some men, including us, return to being men. Only one man in particular now has a new name: he is called the Unique, the man who is unique in his species.

Having discovered that in man negation was power, Sade claimed to found man's future on extreme negation. To reach this point of extreme negation, he came up with a principle—borrowing from the vocabulary of his time—which, by its very ambiguity, illustrates a very ingenious choice. This principle is Energy.

Energy is, in fact, a highly equivocal notion. It is, at once, a reserve and an expenditure of force, an affirmation that is completed only through negation, it is power that is destruction. It is both fact and law, data and value. It is truly striking that, in this universe of effervescence and of passion, Sade, far from designating desire as the highest value, makes it of secondary importance and even judges it suspect. This is because desire denies solitude and leads to a dangerous appreciation of the world of others. But when Saint-Fond declares: "My passions, when concentrated on one particular point, are like rays of light from a star gathered within a magnifying glass: they quickly ignite any object they find in their path," we clearly see how destruction can appear synonymous with power, without the destroyed object eliciting even the slightest value from this operation. Another advantage of this principle: it gives man a future, without imposing on him an awareness of some sort of greater or higher being, without any ideal notion. This is one of Sade's merits. He has claimed to knock the morality of the Good out of the heavens, off its pedestal, bringing it down to earth, but, despite a few provocative affirmations, he took great care not to replace it with a Gospel of Evil. When he writes: "Everything is good when it is excessive," we might reproach him for the lack of precision of his principle, but we cannot fault him for wanting to found the supremacy of man on the sovereignty of notions to which he would forever subordinate himself. Here no conduct is considered to be privileged: we can choose to do anything; what matters is that, in doing it, we be able to impose simultaneously the greatest destruction and the greatest affirmation. Essentially, this is truly what happens in Sade's novels. It is not the amount of virtue or vice that determines whether beings are happy or unhappy, but the energy they expend; because, as he writes, "happiness is in keeping with the energy of principles: there would be none of any of it for the being who floats endlessly." Saint-Fond proposes a plan to Juliette to devastate two thirds of France through starvation. She hesitates and is frightened: immediately, she is threatened. Why? Because she is living proof of weakness, the tenor of her being has diminished, and Saint-

Fond's greater energy is prepared to make her his victim. This is even more clear in the case of Durand. Durand poisons; she is incapable of the slightest virtue; her corruption is absolute. But then one day the government of Venice asks her to spread plague. The project frightens her, not because of its immorality, but because she fears the risks that she herself might run. Immediately, she is condemned. She does not have the energy; she found her master, and her master is death. When leading a dangerous life, says Sade, what is important is to never "lack the necessary strength to surmount the final limits." We might say that this strange world is not comprised of individuals, but of systems of forces, of more or less elevated tension. Catastrophe is therefore inevitable. Furthermore, it is not necessary to distinguish the difference between the energy of nature and man's energy: lust is a kind of lightning bolt, since lightning is nature's lewdness; the weak will be the victim of both, and the strong will emerge triumphant. Justine is struck down, Juliette is not; there is no providential arrangement in this denouement. Justine's weakness serves as an appeal to the same lightning which Juliette's energy deflects away from her. Similarly, everything that happens to Justine makes her unhappy, because everything that affects her diminishes her; about her, we are told that her inclinations were *virtuous but base*, and this must be taken literally. To the contrary, everything that happens to Juliette reveals her power, and she takes pleasure in it as an expansion of herself. This is why, if she were to die, her death would draw her to the limit of power and exaltation, thus allowing her to experience total destruction as the total expenditure of her immense energy.

Sade completely understood that man's energetic sovereignty, to the extent that man acquires this sovereignty by identifying with the spirit of negation, is a paradoxical state. The complete man, completely affirmed, is also completely destroyed. He is the man of all passions and he is unfeeling. He began by destroying himself, first insofar as he was man, then as God, and then as Nature, and thus he became the Unique. Now he can do everything, for the negation in him overthrew everything. To account for its formation, Sade resorts to a highly coherent concept which he gives the classical name of "apathy." Apathy is the spirit of negation applied to the man who has chosen to be sovereign. It is, in a certain way, the cause and the principle of energy. Sade's argument advances approximately in this way: today's individual represents a certain amount of force; most of the time, he disperses his forces, alienating them for the benefit of these simulacrums which are other people, God, ideals. Through this dispersion, he makes the mistake of exhausting his possibilities, wasting them, but even more of founding his behavior on weakness, for if he exhausts his energy for others, he does so because he believes he needs their support. A fatal mistake: he is weakened by vainly expending his forces because he believes himself to be weak. But the true man knows that he is alone and he accepts this; he renounces everything within himself that exists only in relationship to others, to a tradition of seventeen centuries of cowardliness; for example, pity, gratitude, and love are all feelings he destroys; by destroying them, he amasses together all the strength he would have had to consecrate to these debilitating impulses and, what is even more important, from this destructive work he draws the beginning of a true energy.

It is indeed necessary to fully comprehend that apathy does not only consist in ruining "parasitic" affections, but also in opposing the spontaneity of any passion whatsoever. The lecherous man who immediately gives in to his vice is but a runt that will be sacrificed. Even gifted debauchees, perfectly skilled at becoming monsters, if they are happy giving in to their weaknesses, will be destined for catastrophe. Sade is emphatic on this point: for passion to become energy, it is necessary that it be constricted, that it be mediated by passing through a necessary moment of insensibility; then it will be the greatest passion possible. In the initial stages of her career, Juliette was continually scolded by Clairwell: he reproaches her for only committing crimes with enthusiasm, since she thereby ignites the flame of crime only from the flame of passion, she places lust, the effervescence of pleasure, above everything. These are dangerous potentialities. Crime matters more than lust, and the cold-blooded crime is valued more than the crime committed in the heat of the moment; but what matters more than anything is the dark and secret crime "committed by hardening one's sensitive parts," because it is the act of a soul that, having destroyed everything within itself, accumulated enormous force, which will be identified with the move toward total destruction that it prepares. All the great libertines, who live only for pleasure, are great only because they have obliterated within them every capacity for pleasure. This is why they resort to frightening anomalies: otherwise the mediocrity of ordinary voluptuousness would be enough for them. But they have become unfeeling: they expect to find pleasure in their insensitivity, in this rejected sensitivity, and they become ferocious. Cruelty is only the negation of the self, carried so far that it is transformed into a destructive explosion; insensitivity makes the entire being tremble, says Sade; "the soul transforms into a form of apathy which is soon metamorphosed into pleasures a thousand times more divine than the ones that pander to their weaknesses."

We understand that, in this world, principles play a major role. The libertine is "thoughtful, self-contained, incapable of being moved by just anything." He is solitary, does not put up with noise or laughter; nothing must distract him; "apathy, indifference, stoicism, the solitude of the self, these are the conditions necessary for him to attain his proper soul." Such a transformation, such a self-destructive work is not accomplished without extreme difficulty. *Juliette* is a kind of *Bildungsroman*, an instructional manual that teaches us to recognize the slow formation of an energetic soul. Apparently, Juliette is, from the beginning, completely depraved. But in reality she has only a few penchants and her head is intact; there still remains an enormous effort for her to make, because, as Balzac says, *a person who desires cannot be destroyed.* Sade points out that there are very dangerous moments in working toward apathy. For example, it happens that insensitivity sometimes puts the debauchee in such an obliterated state of mind that he could very easily, at this moment, return to moral living: he thinks he is hardened, that he is only weakness, a dupe fully primed for remorse; or one lone virtuous impulse, revalidating the universe of man and God, is enough to overturn all his power; as elevated as he might be, he collapses and, generally, this fall is his death. On the other hand, if in this prostrated state, wherein he experiences only a feeling of bland repugnance for the worst excesses, he musters up one final surge of force in order to augment this insensibility by inventing new excesses that repulse him even more, then he will shift from an obliterated state to an omnipotent one, from hardening and insensitivity to the most extreme pleasure and, "moved at the very core of his being," he will sovereignly delight himself beyond all limits.

One of the surprising aspects of Sade and of his destiny is that, although there is no better symbol of scandal than he, the entirety of the scandalous audacity of his thought has remained long unknown. It is unnecessary to enumerate themes that he discovered that even the most daring minds of centuries to come will employ all their audacity toward reaffirming: we acknowledged them in passing, and yet we restricted ourselves to the task of laying bare the development of Sade's thought by highlighting its essential points. We might just as easily have chosen his conception of the dream, wherein he sees the mind working to return to its instincts and escaping the morality of the day—or of all his thoughts that outstrip Freud's, let's take this one for example: "It is in the mother's womb that organs are made. This must necessarily make us susceptible to some fantasies; the first objects presented to us, the first discussions heard, end in delineating its territory; although we go to school, it changes nothing at all." There exists in Sade a purely traditional moralist, and it would be easy to assemble a selection of his maxims which would make those of La Rochefoucauld appear weak and uncertain. We reproach him for writing badly and he does indeed often write in haste and with a prolixity that exhausts our patience. But he is also capable of a bizarre humor, his style reaches a glacial joviality, a sort of cold innocence within his excesses, which we prefer to all of Voltaire's irony and which is found in no other French writer. All these merits are exceptional, but they have been useless. Until the day when

Apollinaire, Maurice Heine, and André Breton—with his insight-ful conception of the hidden forces of history—opened the way toward him, and even later, until the latest writings of Georges Bataille, Jean Paulhan, and Pierre Klossowski, Sade—master of the major trends of thought and of the modern sensibility—contin-ued to radiate like an empty name. Why? It is because his thought is the work of madness, because it had as its mold a depravity that the world was not ready to face. Additionally, Sade's thought is presented as the theory of this depravity, it is its carbon copy, it claims to transpose the most repugnant anomaly into a complete world view. For the first time, before the eyes of the world, phi-losophy has been conceived as the product of illness,[6] and it shamelessly affirms as universally logical thought a system whose only caution is the preference of an aberrant individual.

This is another one of Sade's most characteristic features. We can say that he performed his own therapy through writing a text in which he confines all his references to his obsessions and where-in he searches for the kind of coherence and the kind of logic that his obsessive remarks reveal. Yet, on the other hand, he was the first to prove, and to do so with pride, that from a certain person-al and even monstrous way of behaving he might rightfully gain a rather significant view of the world, which even great thinkers of the day, scrambling solely to find the meaning of the human con-dition, were able to do nothing more than reaffirm in its main per-spectives and back up its validity. Sade had been brazen enough to affirm that, while courageously accepting his peculiar tastes and assuming them to be the point of departure and the principle for all reason, he was giving philosophy the firmest foundation that he could fathom, and he began to interpret human destiny in its entirety in a profound way. Such a pretension is undoubtedly no longer held to frighten us, but we are only just beginning to take it seriously and, for a long time, this pretension was enough to keep even those who were interested in Sade at a distance.

Firstly, what was he? A monstrous exception, completely out-side humanity. "Sade's uniqueness," Nodier said, "is having com-mitted such a monstrous offense that we have been unable even to characterize it as safe." (Which, in some way, was in fact one of Sade's ambitions: to be innocent through culpability; to use his excessiveness to smash apart, for good, the norm, the laws which could have judged him.) Another of his contemporaries, Pitou, writes in a rather frightening way: "Justice had relegated him to a prison corner giving every prisoner permission to rid the world of this burden." When we then saw in him the example of an anomaly also found in certain individuals, we rushed to shut him up in this unnameable aberration, for which only this unique name seemed to be suitable. Even later, when we made Sade merit this anomaly, when we saw him as a rather liberated man for having invented a new knowledge and, in every way, an exceptional man in both his destiny and his preoccupations, when, finally, in sadism, we saw something possibly of interest to all of humanity, still we continued to neglect his thought, as if we had been sure that there was more originality and authenticity in sadism than in the way Sade himself was able to interpret it. Now, upon closer inspection, it is clear that this thought is essential and that, even surrounded by contradictions, it evolves, it brings us, through the problem illustrated by the name Sade, views more significant than anything the most astute and lucid thought has been able to conceive, even to this day. We are not saying that this thought is viable. But it does show us that between the normal man who locks the sadistic man up in an impasse and the sadistic man who turns this impasse into an escape hatch, the latter is the one who is nearer to the truth, who understands the logic of his situation, and who has a deeper intelligence, to the point of being able to help the normal man understand himself, by helping him modify the foundations of all perception.

The Experience of Lautréamont

No ... let us lead the haggard mattock-and-trench mob no
deeper through the exposable mines of this impious canto!
    —*Maldoror*

... the author hopes that the reader infers ...
    —*Poésies*

The Demand for Separation

Can one comment on *Maldoror*? Undoubtedly. Every com-
mentary on an important work is necessarily at fault in relation to
that work, but commentary is inevitable. The feeling is inevitable
that, sooner or later, propels the reader before that which he most
admires, to substitute himself for that which he admires, to secret-
ly believe himself a little more erudite than the work, a little more
real than the author, due to the fact that the work completes itself
in him and depends on his reasons for admiring it, reasons which
are themselves a product of the times and his own work.

In the presence of a tree resembling the tree of life, the com-
mentator—a particularly suspect character—hastens to pluck its
best fruit, so that the substance and the flavor of this singular
thing having melted in his mouth he might be able to find in its
place a knowledge in which he delights even more, as if therein he
had a superior kind of fruit, one born of him and capable of giv-
ing him the power to recreate, should he so desire, the tree itself.
In the state of original sin, the commentator would therefore
bring with him a flaw; but which one? This is not so clear. Would
it be that of wanting to penetrate the secrets of "life," of asking
creation for the power to do it again? Today this temptation has
truly faded: we ourselves forget it, but the only arrogant ages are
the classical ages, wherein the authors of *art poétique*, perfectly

43

clear on the rules and problems of composition, are very near to believing themselves to be masters of the secret of creation. Such arrogance is paid for by a methodical abasement of the creative act. But today we are far from this pretension and the commentator, rather than explaining how one easily writes great books, feels the necessity to provoke, around completed works, all the problems that make these works impossible to create. After all, a commentator is capable of humility. He can hope to disappear behind what he reveals. He would love to be a reader who is absent from his reading, a barely visible presence, the most modest and reduced that it is possible to be, to the point of becoming, not the eye of the stranger that judges, gauges, defines and does away with what he sees, but the thing itself augmented by a gaze.

Unfortunately, herein lies his error. Clearly, one must consider reading as necessary to the work. But here a reader appears who, inasmuch as he reads, also writes, and, suspending the interior movement through which he gives meaning, life, and freedom to a reality composed of words, substitutes therein new written relations, a system of stable expressions destined to forever maintain the moving power of the work from within a perspective where the work stops, so that it appears more manifest, more clear, more simple, in a repose all too similar to death. Naturally, one might say that this death is the life of works, that reading, to be real, needs to pass through the flow of the world, and that commentary, written or oral, is this survival without which reading would be only the vain meeting of a shadow and a transparency. It is true. And this is why, early or late, it is inevitable that commentary come to works as their glory and the disavowal of that glory.

Why comment on a book? To make it more readable. The critic ingeniously obeys the idea that the reader is something very humble, the book something rather elevated and that, in order to bring these two extremes closer together, an intercessor is necessary. The commentator plays a "mixed" role. In the commentator, the reader's passion and the author's overpowering lucidity are united. The commentator has the sovereign passivity of someone who reads and the controlled freedom of someone who writes. The commentator makes himself master of a text by abandoning himself to it (as is proper to good reading) and he liberates himself from it while being submissive to an other that it creates. Ambiguous creature, incomplete and too complete, unhappy hermaphrodite who, in his position as conciliator, often feels condemned to solitude (as, through an abundance of organs, to sterility).

As the reader's delegate, the critic suffers the temptation to anticipate and to prepare the meeting of these two powers at the lowest point; he husbands the idleness of the reader whom he represents; he indulges his horror of the unexpected, his taste for commodities, his right to diversion. This submission to gravity is part of his role, and he resigns himself to it, even if he wants to evade it. One of the scruples that he finds in himself is in fact the following: so that the reading is real and remains what it must be, a sovereign passivity, is it not necessary that the distance between the work and the reader remain the greatest possible distance? Is communication true only insofar as it is done from an infinite distance, when, for two beings, it becomes the perspective of a distancing that brings together, the place of an incommensurable taken for a common measure? From here certain analysts, naively, overvalue obscurity. But what results from this? The transparent work that the commentary renders opaque, far from being confirmed in the august realm where, beyond the reach of easy sentiments, the critic in good faith would like to place it—so that it might be better seen and admired—has, by this so profound and so elevated commentary, nonetheless fallen to earth, into that region common to theoretical reason. Communication is certainly rendered uncomfortable because a perfected system of dams and screens has been substituted for the wrenching power of the work. And this system discomforts the reader all the more because it is on his level and because therein he finds neither the force nor the momentum nor the vertigo to fall and leave himself behind.

In playing his role, the critic, as an approximation of his name would have it—to criticize is to separate, to disjoin—is necessarily a destroyer. He necessarily separates the work. He destroys it, not by seeing it as smaller than it is, but by rendering it visible to itself, by setting it a little behind, in retreat, so that it apperceives itself, by organizing a slight void in the work, a void that is its momentarily fixed meaning, in relation to the times, to tastes, and to ideas. Always at fault in relation to the work, the critic must at least strive to see it in its most important light, to seek the point where it is the greatest, the most true, the richest. This task is the sole justification for the critic. The absolute value of a book? We do not know it, so far are we from recognizing in posterity an ideal power, an infallible Rhadamanthys[1], capable of unmasking the false masterpieces and perpetuating that which is beautiful. Posterity begins with the first reader and the first critic. To the extent that this reader and this critic maintain the work that they read at its highest level, this highest level is momentarily just, it constitutes a point of equilibrium that the course of history will naturally shift, but which will account for it even in dismissing it. Neither a critic nor a reader are ever entirely wrong about a work when they overestimate it, provided that, rather than through vain praise, it be through effort, even exaggerated effort, to recognize therein the work of an important truth. Undoubtedly, the critic has the right not to like many books. But to denigrate them? Why? Bad works do not equal all the faults that one says of them, nor every fault that offers itself to be said. Even speaking about it is too much.

It is true that, of the books that he loves best, the critic also prefers not to speak. Because he does not always have the desire to distance himself from them, to engage them in this strange work through which he destroys them while realizing them; he diminishes them while exalting them, he simplifies them while deepening them, he gives them so much meaning that the author is surprised and annoyed by this unknown richness, and plaintively protests against a generosity that effaces him and reduces him to nothing. The critic, because of this, is by nature on the side of silence, knowing better than others why he loses what he uncovers and how much the reading of what is most dear to him will become difficult for him, since it will be necessary for him to recover, there, the sad movement of his own sentences.

Lucidity, Darkness

A time always comes when even the most closed books are opened. For a long time *Maldoror*, more admired than commented upon, known but not explained, defied surprise, and for a reason that is at the heart of such a work. Because reading it supposes the exalted consent to a furious lucidity, of which the enveloping movement, pursuing itself without truce, lets itself be recognized only at its end and as the accomplishment of an absolute meaning, indifferent to all the momentary meanings through which moreover the reader must pass so as to attain the repose of a supreme, total signification. An already singular movement. But reading the book is stranger still. There are many others, of which the meaning, hidden from the ideal clarity of words, is only the final obsessive fear, impressive and haunting, of a power in discord with all possible meanings. In these works, rupture is nearly effected with discourse, a manifest rupture, therefore dangerous, because, exaggeratedly visible, it absorbs all attention and becomes the end rather than the principle of a new reason. But *Maldoror* is, in all its parts, full of meaning. There is no phrase that is not clear, no development that is not linked: no special effect, no leap; the same strangeness of figures and bizarreness of scenes depends on motives that are shown to us. The reader, far from seeing himself undone by continuities formed without his awareness, which he would suffer through without understanding, is surrounded by a superior vigilance, always ready to respond to him if asked for a reason, always present if he wants to see it, and which at the same time makes him forget himself so completely that the passion of reading appears here to drag him uncontrollably toward a radical change, toward an exit at the end of which in its being read will substitute the entirely new act of a being, profoundly foreign to the ambition of understanding.

Reading *Maldoror* is a vertigo. This vertigo seems to be the effect of an acceleration of movement that, just like the encircling of fire, at the center of which we find ourselves, provides the impression of a flamboyant void or of an inert and somber plenitude. Sometimes we see ourselves at the heart of an exceptionally active, sarcastic consciousness that it is hardly possible to fault. Sometimes this omnipresent agility, this whirlwind of lightning bolts, this storm overloaded with meaning, no longer offers the idea of a spirit in any way, but of a lumbering, blind instinct, of a dense thing, of this tenacious heaviness, proper to the body that undoes itself and to substances seized by death. These two impressions are superimposed; they necessarily go together. They give the reader a drunkenness that races to its fall and an inertia docile at his stagnation. In these conditions, how could he have the desire, and the means, to regain enough equilibrium to discern where he is falling? He proceeds and he sinks. Therein is his commentary.

One must not therefore misunderstand the remarks that follow. They do not constitute a search for the "true" meaning of *Maldoror*, nor even an attempt to interrogate what the work says while countering it insidiously with itself. We would simply like to prove to what extent one can follow a text and at the same time lose it, being at once the one who understands and the one who understands him, man, inside a world, who speaks about it as if he were outside; in sum, to profit from the bizarreness of a double work and of an author split in two, absolute lucidity and thick darkness, consciousness that knows everything and knows not where it goes, so as to feign the illusion of a commentary entirely conscious of not being able to explain anything and at the same time uniquely preoccupied with making everything reasonable.

Roger Caillois puts it well at the beginning of his essay: "Here is a work that contains its own commentary."[2] And he rightly adds: "It is also very difficult to talk about." But the third sentence opens a reflection: "More precisely, the author has already said everything that one can say, and in this same work." Perhaps. At the same time, if the "lucidity" of Lautréamont is so great, if it is "admirable," it cannot ignore that this interior commentary that it offers us, present in a way that is visible in many passages and again apparent when it does not appear, in such a way that it seems to pump life into the entire work, like mercury flowing by leaps and by capriciousness, like a substance that would be infinitely lively and yet heavier than blood, this commentary that is part of the work cannot serve to judge it or to define it "exactly," because it helps shape it, therein modifying it, and since this chance, this progressive transformation that it provokes, changes its very own bearing and strips all its power to reveal to us the final character of a work at the heart of which it is seized. The "judgments," the "expressions" we find in *Maldoror* cannot be "precise" because even if one only wants to see them as sarcastic streaks designed to open a view, while lacerating what is revealed, one must now take into account these streaks through which the lacerations completely modify the value of the images, recognize this "exactitude," necessarily false because it cannot recognize itself. It is certainly probable that Lautréamont's clairvoyance was also the clairvoyance of a critical judgment. We find proof of this in the *Poésies*, not in the parts where he condemns his work, but in those where he defines it. There we see that this author has not ignored what he has done, nor how he did it. But if his irony is the lucidity of a writer capable of distancing himself with respect to what he writes and of momentarily setting it apart with a ruse, it is even more sure that these differences, these voids, this absence, do not constitute *clarifications* of the work without a relation to it, but are the work itself and, by these means, unite it with entirely contrary movements. What would Lautréamont's lucidity be if it had not been discerned in all these "precise" judgments, incorporated in certain sentences as similar phrases inverted, a power of indefinite falsification that falsifies these judgments and eliminates from them every power to thoughtfully skim them?

In *The Cantos*, he tells us, "Everything is explained, important details as well as minor ones" (147). A sentence that would be a supreme hoot if the impression was that everything is said, that "the secret is discovered" (as he again affirms it), that what would otherwise be dissimulated here divulges itself. This impression was in fact so vivid that one comes to want to interrogate the text from every angle for the sole pleasure of hearing it respond. Regardless of this temptation, the interpreter can only defend himself by invoking Lautréamont against himself. At the end of the second

Canto, there is a troubling morsel that the commentator can hardly forget: "No ... ," Maldoror says, "let us lead the haggard mattock-and-trench mob no deeper through the exposable mines of this impious canto! The crocodile will change not a word of the vomit that gushed from his cranium" (105). What critic would not feel targeted by such a furious echo, such a direct response to the question that prevents all others? And at the same time, how can he account for this warning? Here, to recognize a response legitimately given by Maldoror on *Maldoror* is also to recognize that the interrogation is legitimate. It is therefore to accept entrance into the "impious" task of excavation that is all analysis, and to yield to the desire to believe that if in fact "everything is explained," even this must be: everything must not be explained. For the critic, the outcome is inevitable, and he who resists the temptation has already succumbed.

The Mirage of Sources: *The Book of Revelation*[3]

Often the obscurity of a work is protected by our ignorance of its sources. One sees in the work a meteor without origin, a trace of fire without any hearth. But the "literary" sources of the *Cantos* are perfectly known to us, "explained" by Lautréamont himself. We know extremely well where his book is coming from: "I have sung of evil as did Mickiewicz, Byron, Milton, Southey, A. de Musset, Baudelaire, etc."[4] H. R. Linder, in an occasionally surprising but meticulous and attentive work, discovered a new source: *The Book of Revelation.*[5] "Black Revelation," he says of *Maldoror.* Linder demonstrates that the strangeness of this character comes, in part, from the dark visions of St. John the Divine and from the naive way he incarnates various apocalyptic apparitions. Maldoror is at once Satan, the enemy of God and the Angel of the abyss, who represents God's anger, and the Horseman of the Apocalypse, divine scourge sent to punish man's guilty rebellion. From this superimposition of contrary meanings, Lautréamont obtains the ambiguous character of his symbolic figure.

This is an interpretation that Lautréamont authorizes, since he talks about this subject nearly as much as his interpreter does. In numerous passages, Maldoror identifies himself with the Prince of Darkness, being of "divine essence," inhabiting superior spheres, and being more powerful than the great Satan himself.[6] In other cases, he presents himself as a Horseman of the Apocalypse.[7] Elsewhere still, he is more a punishment for the rebellious man than the motivating force of his rebellion.[8] All of these various roles need not be uncovered: they are openly affirmed. As for the game of echoes, each of us can give ourselves to it endlessly: it is a matter of reading, of knowledge and ingenuity. According to Linder, the stanza of the "pact with prostitution," canto I, was directly inspired by the famous passage in *Revelation* on the "Great Whore," the one "who is seated on many waters," "Babylon the great, mother of whores and of earth's abominations."[9] The battle between the dragon and the eagle evokes the image of the Beast that received "power, the throne, prestige" from the "Dragon," the name of which is the mysterious, human number 666, or, according to certain manuscripts, 616.[10] The louse of canto II would only be a modern variation of the scourge of locusts, called forth by the trumpet of the fifth angel (Rev 9: 3). Let's admit it.[11]

But how can we stop ourselves once on this path? Who would prevent us from seeing, in our turn, the cruel repast of the Creator (75–78) as a recollection of the verse in John where the angel summons the birds and says to them: "Come, gather for the great supper of God, to eat the flesh of kings, the flesh of captains, the flesh of the mighty, the flesh of horses and of their riders—flesh of all, free and slave, small and great" (Rev 19: 17–19). In *Poésies*, Lautréamont refers us more precisely to cruel Indian divinities, to Moloch, to the "manitous Manicheans, soiled with brains, who *ferment*[12] the blood of their victims in the sacred pagodas of the Hindustan," to the "snake," the "toad," the "crocodile," "divinities, considered abnormal, by ancient Egypt," "Viscous Gods vomited by the primitive imagination of the barbarous peoples."

Nevertheless, even while admitting that Lautréamont is inspired by *Revelation* and that, for example, his dragon might really be a reincarnation of the Beast, it is still necessary to notice, in

Maldoror, a constant exchange between the two powers, top and bottom; now it is God who is the Beast, and he does not stop groveling. Maldoror is, effectively, rarely a snake (we are told of his scales a few times[13]), but God sometimes becomes a dragon, sometimes a snake, and is finally an "eccentric python," a boa with a "triangular head" who has all the characteristics of the ancient snake.[14] In this same stanza, there is a great temptation to search for scattered features of inverted images from *Revelation*. One remembers that, in St. John, "the great dragon, the ancient serpent, who is called the Devil and Satan" (Rev 12:9), projected on earth, pursues the Woman, who, with her son, escapes into the desert where the Beast plans to devour her (Rev 17:16). But Maldoror says to the python (that is, to God): "You had better retreat before me and go and wash your immeasurable shame in the blood of a newborn child: such are your habits. . . . Cross desert sands till the end of the world swallows up the stars in nothingness" (172). And, to carry these conjectures to their end, notice again in "my young wife and my very young son" that Maldoror advises his adversary to live from the shards of memories drifting and detached from the same tableau.

Baudelaire

Whether or not images from *Revelation* bounced around in Lautréamont's head may perhaps be important, but the images themselves are less important than the reversal that they undergo herein, where the intended mockery, though immediately visible, fails to account for them. On this point, the critic surely has much to say. But since we are at the source of these images, why does H. R. Linder—who, while exaggerating Maldoror's Luciferian stature, seems to be at a loss to explain its origin, so much so that he returns to *Revelation* each time he perceives a demonic shadow on the character in question—why does he not move a bit closer: not only to Milton (whom Lautréamont mentions), to Byron (whom he also mentions), or to Lewis, but to Baudelaire, who transformed Satan into such a dynamic poetic figure that any young imagination at the time, if it wanted to return to the mythic, ancient rebellion, could not fail to pass through *The Flowers of Evil*? Does this need to be proven? Anyone who was twenty years old in 1865 and had his head in the clouds, dreaming of almighty evil, must necessarily reach for the works of Baudelaire, wherein is breathed the most intense satanic density in our literature. And, for Lautréamont, Baudelaire is not only a source of principles, but a hall of memories; any attentive reading would show it. The famous stanza about the ocean is haunted by the memory of "L'Homme et la Mer" ("Man and the Sea"). If we consult the text, we find the image of the ocean's "discretion": "You are both dark and discreet," says Baudelaire; "You are modest," says Lautréamont (38). Then *Maldoror*'s shift to parody begins: "Yes, which is the deeper, the more impenetrable of the two: the ocean or the human heart?" (40). And Baudelaire:

> Man, no one's ever plumbed the depths of your abyss,
> O sea, no one can know your hidden treasury,
> You both preserve your secrets with such jealousy!

"I detest you," says Lautréamont. "I hate you, Ocean!" says Baudelaire ("Obsession"). "Answer me, ocean," says Lautréamont, "do you want to be my brother?" Baudelaire:

> Free man, beside the sea that you'll forever cherish!
>   ...
> O you eternal wrestlers, O brothers without peace!

Certainly, the similarities would seem to be numerous. In the stanza on prostitution, Hans Linder sees a recollection of "the Great Prostitute." With good reason, perhaps. But regardless of whether he is recalling the sonnet *"Remords posthume"* ("Posthumous Remorse"), he will see therein the exact setting of that stanza: the tomb, the beautiful woman whose name is Prostitution ("My lovely, dusky slave," says Baudelaire, "flawed courtesan"), and, finally, the "worm" that appears in both texts as the powerful adversary of beauty and, representing God, maintains moral discourse (in *"Remords posthume,"* the tomb speaks, but in Lautréamont, the worm in a certain way becomes the tomb: it is "large like a house," and, if it glows, it is with "an immense light of blood"). Naturally, from one text to the other, the changes are significant, but we never hear it proven that Lautréamont, putting to work his theory of plagiarism, took the resources of his invention from a precursor. The contrary is more likely. There where we surprise him in the flagrant delight of reminiscence is also where the strangeness of his work explodes, along with the unique power of his vision and the singular workings of his lucidity. Having voiced this reservation, if we recall this passage—"One should let one's fingernails grow for a fortnight. Oh! how sweet to snatch brutally from his bed a boy who has yet nothing upon his upper lip ... And all of a sudden, just when he least expects it, to sink your long nails into his tender breast ... " (31)— how can we not invoke this image from "Bénédiction" ("Benediction"):

> When I am finally bored with impious mockery,
> I'll occupy my frail and forceful hand with sport:
> A harpy's fingernails my fingernails will be
> To excavate a trough into his very heart.

The gallows of "Un Voyage à Cythère" ("A Voyage to Cythera"), itself taken from Gérard de Nerval, can hardly be forgotten when we consider the terrible gallows in canto IV, from which a man is hung by his hair. Lautréamont was unquestionably capable of finding such an image on his own and developing it according to the fluctuations of his desire. But the correspondence established by Baudelaire, between the "ghost of the ancient Venus" (of womanly love) and the hanging body devoured by birds, reappears verbatim in the pages of *Maldoror*. We must see it as an obsession sustained in common. It is impossible that an imagination as extremely aware of animal metamorphoses as Ducasse's had not been inspired by such verses:

> A few ferocious birds were perched on their reflection
> And in a rage destroyed a corpse already foul;
> Each used a filthy beak for gouging like a tool
> Into each bloody cranny of the putrefaction.

The eyes were two bleak holes, and through the ruined skin
The ponderous intestines dangled on the thighs.
His executioners, gorged on their hideous prize,
With snappings of the beak slowly castrated him.

Lautréamont's hanged man also grapples with the misfortune of castration and the punishment of impotence. And Maldoror, for this wretched man whom he saves and cares for with perfect charity, feels the inklings of a mysterious sympathy, the same sympathy that Baudelaire expresses:

Ridiculous cadaver, your sorrows are my own!

Still more on the mirage of sources: In the episode on God's repast, we wanted to see an allusion to *Revelations*, then, according to Lautréamont, an allusion to oriental mythology.[15] But now we would also discover therein a recollection of the following stanzas from "Reniement de saint Pierre" ("St. Peter's Denial"):

What does God do about the flood of obloquy
That rises every day around his Seraphim?
Like a good tyrant gorged on wine and venison,
He falls asleep to the sweet sounds of our blasphemy.[16]

The sobs of martyrs and the beaten felon's cry
Provide intoxicating symphonies, no doubt;
Despite the spate of blood spilled at their sensuous bout,
The heavens never have enough to satisfy!

But if we recall that the same grim cannibalism gave way to a classic scene in Dante's *Inferno* (and Maldoror's imagination, we have acknowledged, loves to see heaven where others put hell), if we remember that Malraux seized upon the origins of the same vision in a very popular English engraving from 1860, *The Red Devil*—an image that, through the same impulse, Ducasse would have turned precisely on its head, substituting God for the Demon—if we recall these things, we will perhaps be tempted to take the search for references and faith in the importance of beginnings for an illusion. A prudent conclusion, though, too, possibly deceptive. To discover ten sources for one image and to accept them all is, in itself, more reasonable than giving credit to only one. The delirium of "interpretation," to which every interpreter occasionally falls prey, begins with the need to restore reason, through one single principle or through a concurrent system of causes, to all the details or to the greatest number of possible fluctuations, to words and figures, as if the solemn unity of the work did not distort this multiplicity on the basis of which we claim to verify it, or as if the precision of the explanation was not, according to a certain measure (but by what measure?), guaranteed by its failure and the reservation that secretly arranges therein the moment of its disavowal. And yet this last precaution must also seem suspect, because an interpretation, capable of explaining everything, even everything that cannot be explained, testifies to such an implacable will to clarify everything that we must recognize herein the powerful systematization of desire, which the mind attempts to understand under the name of madness.

If we find ten references behind the same image in *Maldoror*, if these ten archetypes or models are so many masks overlapping and monitoring one another, without any one reference appearing as the true mold of the face it recalls or appearing completely alien to it, this is the sign that Lautréamont was in agreement with the few rare points of the space where the collective power of the imagination and the unique power of the book see their resources combined. He who touches upon these points upsets, without knowing it, an infinite number of analogies and of related images, a monumental past of tutelary words toward which he is driven, unbeknownst to him, like a man endorsed by an eternity of fables. And he who knows this, who is familiar with the literary chain of certain figures, is, due to the fact that he touches these points, led beyond all the certainties of his personal memory and seized by an impulse that transforms him into the agent for a knowledge that he never had.

Lautréamont was undoubtedly a cultivated adolescent. He passionately read all the works that life in his day made great and fascinating. His imagination is surrounded by books. And yet, as far as possible from being bookish, this imagination seems to pass through books only to reconnect with the great constellations of which the books guard the influence, bundles of impersonal imagination that no single author's work can halt or monopolize to his or her advantage. It is shocking that Lautréamont, even if he follows the trend of his time, even when he expresses, with the insolence of youth, biases and circumstantial passions, the glorification of evil, a taste for the gruesome, a Luciferian challenge, he undoubtedly does not betray these sources, but, at the same time, seems to be haunted by all the masterpieces from every century, ultimately appearing as if he were meandering in a world of fiction wherein vague dreams of forgotten religions and mythologies, shaped by everything and destined for everything, reconnect and are confirmed.

If, when he talks about Satan, we judge him to be inspired by *Revelation* rather than by Baudelaire, this error in perception is just, because it reveals that, without knowing the literary invention unique to *The Flowers of Evil*, it resurfaced, across Baudelaire, through the power peculiar to this image of Satan, in the kingdom of myths that opens up at the beginning and the end of the story.[17] And if Malraux perceives, beneath such a scene, not a literary model, but the visual influence of a painting, even if Lautréamont never knew *The Red Devil* and if on the contrary he was subjected to the counter-shock of a poetical text, the power of the *image* never ceases to be at work in him, the power by which words are detached, detached from their temporal origin, from the memories that animate books, and caught up within the movement of an immense dream memory, the plastic mother of nightmares and of certain paintings.

In Search of a Method of Exploration

One might refuse to descend into *Maldoror* due to the fact that no analysis of it is possible. What might an analysis attain? A story? No one wants this, and besides, except for canto VI, there isn't any. A subject? But the subject, if we isolate it in order to grasp it, if we reduce it to some kind of Manichean struggle, is a

simple theoretical reflection that disregards the entirety of the pro-
found life of the work. No one is interested in that. So, a method-
ical search for the content of scenes, for the meaning that rumbles
therein, for the sensibility that comes to light? We would, for
instance, bring up a sentence: "I set my genius to portray the
pleasures of cruelty!" (29). Then we would search anew for all the
declarations that refer back to this phrase: "Innate cruelty whose
suppression does not lie with me"—"an extreme and instinctive
cruelty of which he himself is ashamed"—"I was not as cruel as
has been recounted, among men," etc. From this perspective, one
would first examine all the episodes: all the scenes wherein a
schema manifesting cruelty appears (the razor that lacerates a face,
the nails that dig into a chest, the little girl thrown against a wall
or threatened with such, the castaway blown apart by two gun-
shots, etc.), those scenes wherein the cruel intention is also obvi-
ously an erotic one (the attack with the bulldog, the attack on the
world in the stanza about pederasts), the scenes wherein the erot-
ic cruelty dissimulates itself beneath nearly transparent forms (all
of active or imagined violence against amiable adolescents: Falmer,
Elseneur, Reginald, Mervyn). After this first attempt, we would
file away all the devastating scenes and barbaric acts, initiated by
others and condemned by Maldoror: divine ferocity (God's cruel
repast, the stanza about the red lantern and the young man tor-
mented to death by God), the cold malice of men (the stanza
about the omnibus), the erotic viciousness of women (the torture
of the hanged man, the beetle's misfortunes). Then, shifting from
the scenes in general to their details, from episodes to images, we
would see that in addition to the pleasure Maldoror feels when evil
is inflicted on others, he nearly always expresses either moral
malaise, regret, shameful repentance, or a strange thirst for for-
giveness. (For example, at the end of the stanza about the finger-
nails: "I know that your forgiveness was as immense as the uni-
verse"; after the evocation of violent acts against the young girl:
"The unknown was not able to keep its forces and faded away";
after the attack on Falmer: "How benevolent his voice is. . . . Has
he therefore forgiven me?," etc.) Moreover, it seems that if

Maldoror inflicts harm, he immediately feels the need to harm himself: he had barely finished ripping a child apart when he dreamt of being torn apart by that child himself. "For you will rend me incessantly with both teeth and nails . . . ; and together we shall suffer, you through tearing me apart, I through being torn apart . . . " (32–33). He is as much the one who is wounded as the one who wounds. The blood that spills forth reminds him of his own blood, the tears that he makes fall taste like his own. Who is the victim? Who the executioner? The ambiguity is perfect. Sometimes the pleasure of atonement is concealed, but for even more shocking research: here Maldoror watches a shipwreck, the screams, the moaning from this immense misfortune thrill him. He seems to be at the height of pleasure; but what does he do? "Every quarter of an hour or so, whenever a gust of wind, stronger than the rest, keening its dismal dirge amid the cries of startled petrels, struck and cracked the ship's length and increased the moans of those about to be offered up to death-by-holocaust, I would jab a sharp iron point into my cheek, secretly thinking: 'They suffer still more!' Thus, at least, I had grounds for comparison" (96). An admirable digression. The same perspective could accommodate the various episodes wherein we see Maldoror hurting himself while struggling with another, as when, striking down the Dragon, he strikes down Hope within himself, as when, in several scenes, wherein the mirror's deception intervenes, he forgets to recognize himself in the reflected image and continues with his accusations, through a misunderstanding that, at that moment, reveals that his sarcastic remarks and violent acts are destined for none other than Maldoror himself.[18]

Continuing this inquiry, we would uncover the scenes, the images wherein cruelty is initially inflicted upon others (then reprimanded in others), but is observed within them with an at once complicit and indignant complacency, before (or simultaneously as) this cruelty is turned against Maldoror by Maldoror himself, either to punish himself, or to make himself feel good, or to make himself feel good in punishing himself, or finally to suggest the continual lies of the sensibility—because the other person is nec-

essarily me—this violent, stunning cruelty falls back into a dismal
suffering, becomes an indefinite sinking, without pleasure or out-
rage. Of this suffering, the monumental image is that of Maldoror,
stuck within the immobility of a tree, permitting himself to be
slowly devoured by monsters "issued from the kingdom of viscos-
ity." The figure evokes Job, but replaces Job's demanding power,
his frenetic faith in the effectiveness of misfortune, with an unspo-
ken wish for inertia and death.[19] And yet, within this immense
passivity, the flame of an active consent persists, remains capable
of overturning, when the time comes, all this suffering through
revolt: "Hate is stranger than you think ... Even as you see me
now I can still make forays to the very walls of heaven, heading a
legion of assassins, and return to resume this posture and medi-
tate anew upon lofty plans of vengeance" (143). The image of an
energetic pain also remains, like the reminder of a struggle soon
to recommence: the image of a double-edged sword that a cun-
ning adversary impales vertically up Maldoror's back, along his
spinal column. (Mirage of sources: Kafka described precisely the
same situation in a short story, "The Sword"—"A knight's great
and ancestral sword was embedded up the length of my back to
the hilt, but, without having been able to understand the reason
for it, the blade was slipped in between the skin and flesh without
creating any wound. There wasn't any more left on my neck at the
point where it had penetrated ... "[20]) In *Maldoror*, as in Kafka, the
operation occurs in a strange darkness, a momentary loss of mem-
ory: "I didn't see anything, for a short moment... " But soon there-
after, the power awakens, a quake that shakes both earth and sky:
"This sharp whinyard buried itself to the hilt between the shoul-
der-blades of the fiesta bull, whose frame shuddered like a tremor"
(143). What therefore is this image, if, as the noble beast of com-
bat, it fails to evoke the bull of the holocaust, the bull whose sac-
rifice is the immolation of the supreme power, so that, since the
bull here is Maldoror, one must suspect a deeply ambiguous rela-
tionship between Maldoror and the powers above, as well as
between the evil that one provokes and the evil to which one sub-
mits. The stanza about "the enormous suction-cups," about those

ten years of night through the course of which "the old spider of the great species" keeps the sleeping one under his immobile power, marks an improvement, a completion of this inert suffering. In the case of the tree, there is still consent, secret will, and deviation from hatred, but here the dreamer believes himself to have authorized the nightmare in vain; the permission, granted by the dream, is no more than an illusion denounced in the end.[21] To these two scenes where Maldoror seems to be no more than a suffering passivity or, more precisely, a force, ordered, paralyzed by suffering, we should add the sketches of these scenes (some of them essential) where, struggling with his sleep, he appears behind this sleep that immobilizes him, and some grim scenes wherein, rather than dead, he appears behind his death, his "cadaveresque" existence held by an unusual force equidistant from the possibilities of life and death (but we will encounter these possibilities again later).

What is the value of such analysis? First, it demands that one pursue it to the end. With regard to these digressions on the subject of cruelty, it would be necessary to delineate the course of completely different feelings. Maldoror, who finds his cruelty "delightful," is in fact a character overflowing with good deeds. He corrupts young souls, but he also comes to their defense. He smashes the heads of castaways, but he saves those who are drowning and, after resuscitating them, recognizes them to be precious beings, forgotten friends: a significant reward, for if *Maldoror* carries a moral of bitter pessimism, we could see the fatalism of ingratitude and resentment behind these good deeds. Maldoror is, instinctively, on the side of human kindness (the stanza about the omnibus), on the side of the weak against the strong. If he sees a wretched man, hanging from the gallows and abandoned to every reprisal of feminine desire, though he possibly draws some exquisite pleasure from this remarkable spectacle, in the end he comes to the aid of this unfortunate man, treats him with a nearly maternal gentleness; his concern is extremely serious.[22] Strange hero of evil! Evil is far from his original passion. He often says, in a curious way: Meanness arises in him at the same time as pity; the sight of injustice inspires hate in him, and this hatred pushes him to terrible extremes, of which one by one God, men, and himself are the insufficient victims. Seeing God occupied with his appalling cannibalistic work, he experiences an immense pain, "the feeling of pain that engenders pity for a great injustice"; "With this feeling of pain is joined an intense fury against this maternally cruel tigress, whose hardened cubs know only how to curse and to inflict pain." The only excuse he finds for these criminal acts is the same transference, the same emotional extremes: "I was not as cruel as men later related; but sometimes their wickedness wreaks its enduring ravages for years on end. So my fury knew no limit; I was seized with an access of cruelty and struck awe in anyone (of my own race) who might happen to meet my haggard eyes" (97). Sometimes, it is truly painful for him to lead the war against his own people: "Two friends stubbornly trying to destroy one another, what a drama!" (133). But the combat is inevitable. His sympathy for men who upset his sensibility, the gateway to extreme violence, ambiguous violences which, in light of the hatred they represent, are justified by reflections on universal guilt, but which also have a soft passionate side that condemns him to remorse, making him feel the infinite value of men and the injustice of the evil done to them. In sum, he is ferocious because tender, and pitiless from too much pity.

Let us stop here. Our analysis has brought us to the point where criticism becomes easy.

Undoubtedly, such preliminary work of classification and comparison can at least offer us a certain idea of the sensibility of *Maldoror*. Even when illegitimate, such analytic procedures remain valuable, if we intend to interrogate a work according to the major commonplaces on which life and traditional knowledge turn. For example, the question of Lautréamont's sadism might be raised, it might be hastily settled, with the help of a typical phrase or with only a single scene in mind. Analysis tackles these cursory judgments. It reveals that the theoretical intention that is a general declaration of war, a universal promise of violence, is not in keeping with the particular movements of a work. There certainly are excessively brutal acts, but soon thereafter they are compensated with remorse, with a vigorous affirmation of human generosity and, on a level of the deepest sensibility, with a bizarre transformation that proceeds from suffering—researched and tasted with voluptuous exaltation—to a dark and paralyzing oppression. It is fairly obvious that Maldoror is incapable of sticking with evil, that, once he commits an evil act (which is, in fact, rather rare), he pulls away from it with an uncontrollable movement, a movement that is like the reflux of evil onto him and which he experiences in the double form of repentance and the pleasure of self-laceration. From the point of view of intention, Lautréamont is very far from Sade. In Lautréamont, there is a natural rebellion against injustice, a natural tendency toward goodness, a powerful elation that is, from the start, characterized by neither perversion nor evil. In this, undoubtedly, he is even extremely far from Baudelaire.[23] And yet, it is true that something mysterious must be happening in Lautréamont: in the moment of struggle, he suddenly throws himself utterly into the evil that he forcefully rejects, the evil for which he lacks even the religious soul's consideration as sin, thereby surpassing in excess all the excesses that he condemns. "I am here to defend man," he says. But the outcome of the fighting negates the reason for fighting: the struggle for man's freedom makes man unbearable to him and, becoming his executioner, he crushes man while liberating him.

The Perpetual Movement of Analysis

Now, we understand that commentators have had the choice of searching for the true meaning of *Maldoror* as a poetry of aggressive intoxication, which would be its own end, all narrative justifications, given after the fact, of such elation becoming negligible, or, on the contrary, adhering strictly to the manifest content of the poetry. Gaston Bachelard forcefully chose the first approach, and what he wrote on this subject certainly has tremendous general value, but the focus of his perspective led him to overestimate the brutal impulsions in Lautréamont's work and blinded him to the subterranean life, to the obsession with sleep, to this sympathy, filled with horror, for the "kingdom of viscosity," that plays no less an important role in the text. Thus he could write: "Maldoror is above suffering. He causes rather than undergoes it,"[24] whereas our analysis has just shown us Maldoror practically never induces suffering without receiving it soon thereafter and very often he is the only one who endures suffering, with a stillness not unlike death. "Ducasse's beings do not digest—they bite."[25] As if the world in *Maldoror* was not that of "the immense suction," of the grip of octopuses, of interior absorption. "He is never asleep."[26] Yes, if being asleep is being unaware that one is sleeping; but if sleep is the confining lucidity, if it is the stupor at the bottom of sleep, if it is the dream, how can one not see *Maldoror* as supremely impregnated with sleep, as a work that forcefully represents the tragedy of the paralyzed struggle at the heart of the night? And this is why, again: "In *Maldoror* nothing is simply passive, ... nothing is awaited."[27] This is to neglect the character of endless waiting that is always progressively imposing itself from stanza to stanza and that transforms the first five cantos into an obsessive shuffling back and forth before an always impending and inaccessible resolution.

Hans Rudolf Linder courageously welcomed the thesis of a Lautréamont who knows what he says, of a work wherein the struggle against God is truly a struggle against God, a gigantic struggle to find the secret of being and, finally, to expose the reason for sovereign evil while devoting himself to evil, while forcing evil, with a kind of sympathetic sorcery. An opinion that the commentator eloquently defends, sometimes persuasively, though he pushes it so far that in the end we see Lautréamont's blasphemy change into a glorification of heaven and his insolent fighting into a search for God.[28]

These two commentaries undoubtedly go beyond the movements of our analysis. But precisely this analysis, although it might only have been roughly sketched out and an empty shell, has quickly progressed beyond its prescript and demonstrated a propensity to rethink the work as a whole from an isolated motif within it. The work has in some ways been reviewed with this motif—become its judge—in mind. Around it, our analysis attempted to recompose the work, preferably in a coherent manner, so that the proof might be completed by means of a true center and not an arbitrarily chosen detail.

A dangerous deviation, but one that is able to correct itself by its own impetus. Only the thematic analysis of cruelty leads us to the point where that analysis is no longer enough. We have touched upon the enigmatic moment where Maldoror, simultaneously cruel and tender, rebels against evil and is thrilled to do so. He is dissatisfied if he does evil, but from this dissatisfaction delight is extracted, undirected aggressivity and unwillful passivity taking absolutely no pleasure in causing evil or in enduring evil, no more so than he seems to experience, pointlessly holding on to the reasons for what he does, while nearly always losing sight of them.

We are told that the enigma is short-lived, that the analysis ends in an array of contradictions because it takes everything into account, except for the sarcastic contradiction present in every moment of the work. The seriousness of the analysis, having allowed the absence of the seriousness of the irony to escape, is truly surprised to discover its effects within this accumulation of contradictory thoughts, into which it now looks in vain, after having neglected its principal reason. Irony is, assuredly, a dreadful adversary for analysis, which sees the right to consider each moment separately and to define its content vanish into thin air. Enumeration is no longer possible if the meaning of each detail is coupled with a mocking intention which not only erases it (this is the least of the difficulties), but opens it up in an ambiguous way to an undefined oscillation of improbable meanings. Now, where we see remorse we have possibly forgotten to see a condemnation of remorse, and there where we see remorse become a mockery of itself we do not see the heartbreak that reestablishes, at the heart of sarcasm, the power concealed by remorse. And so on for everything else, endlessly. The powerful marvel of irony: an admirable defense against the peculiarities of discourse and against the investigation of a too simple rationality. But a power that is, however, vulnerable, because it cannot show something truer than itself, more lastingly real than all its infinitely diverse resources; it was only this negative constancy that in the end referred us back to cruelty and moves us toward a new examination of this theme.

Analysis is a machine that is not easily stopped. The difficulties that impede it become for it a new path that it traverses to the end with the certainty of its undeterred gait. Analysis encounters irony, a sort of glimmer of death invented specifically to disrupt mechanisms like its own. But far from letting itself be disturbed by these obstacles, analysis curiously embraces them, counts them, classifies them, and, at the end of this new process, confronts the results of this examination with the previous conclusions, wisely sectioned off, during this work, between parentheses.

Let's assume these results have been clearly established. Admitting that they methodically show us what the briefest reading permits us to understand: that irony is not evenly spread throughout the work, that at times it is certainly nonexistent or at work more than ever, but that it also has its moments of weakness, that at certain times it becomes so tenuous that, like a weak dose of poison, it confirms meaning rather than weakening it. We will also see that irony, rarely a simple critical power, is on the contrary most often an exorbitant way of affirming, an excess where seriousness is undoubtedly displaced, but only in order to regain itself, in this sphere of rupture, in the form of vertigo and of the "joyous cries of nothingness." It is certainly not easy to reconquer the logical elements of an affirmative word within such a dispersal; analysis recognizes this, but, without entering into the details of what rightfully remains of it, analysis maintains, in any case, the general possibility of appreciating the contents of the work, of searching for its meaning from the meaning manifested by certain phrases and by certain stanzas or, if one rejects as valueless the work's immediate meaning—which, we might add, was also mutilated by the clashes of a peculiar composition—of searching for this meaning as it *stems from the consistency of motifs, from an obsession with devices, from the fatal return of words and images, which is to say, of form.*

The commentators therefore find themselves faced with two principal paths, established for them by analysis. Some of them, like H. R. Linder, will think that a work wherein the hero spends most of his time struggling with God has something to do with God and that, since this work, in the opinion of those that enter into it, has an unsettling power and reality, we have the right to want to grasp the highest possibility, dealing with the most tragically important questions for the human condition, that is openly at stake in this work. But others will estimate that the distressing power of this book, clearly at odds with the goals of the discourse that has no care for order, unity, or logical permanence, a book that is a muddle of scenes, words, and images, the effectiveness of which, certainly extraordinary, is perfectly indifferent to the apparent meaning, that such a power will be lost if one continues to place it at the level of the great questions and of the great thoughts that this book has left behind, questions that it perhaps used as a sounding board, but regarding which it presents a furious, prodigious leap, a soaring into the void. If analysis wants to do something useful, it must not look to what Lautréamont said, but to what was expressed behind his words, with the help of this new language made up of choice images, the privileged amassing of words, and the collusion of certain themes. On this level, irony itself ceases to be formidable: we can consider declarations on evil, on God, as dubious. We can also regard as perfectly foreign to Maldoror the actions that are attributed to him as well as the predilections that he fosters: for example, "*I* do not like women! Nor even hermaphrodites! *I* have always taken an infamous fancy to pale youngsters in schools and the sickly mill-children!" (174). But if, in order to implement the inclination of his mockery, he must always appeal to certain figures, if, behind his violence, which constantly smashes affirmation against affirmation, scene against scene, he has no choice but to allow another world to take shape, a world shaped by his preference for such images, by the obsessive attraction that they exert on him, this is proof that his mockery is powerless against certain omnipotent forces, those that are affirmed through words that would like to prevent all affirmation and, behind their logical death, breathe life into imaginary values and motivations. As such we can judge this struggle with God, apparently undertaken to help men, as meaningless, a struggle that leads equally to a continual evocation of God as to a continual explosion against men. But what then becomes meaningful is that, throughout this battle, the work allows itself to be invaded incrementally by an obscure confusion of metamorphosed being, it gives way to marshy phantoms, a pile of octopuses, of toads, of crabs, spiders that hum, leeches that suck blood, countless snakes. Lautréamont's poetry reveals perhaps nothing to someone who naively questions it about God and about evil, but it reveals itself through its tendency to be able to speak about God only by means of fantastical animal figures—and to not talk to us about it, to forget to talk to us about it, while being condensed around thick living substances, which are at once over-abundantly active and of an interminable inertia.

We should say that after all is said and done there is not much of a difference between these two trajectories of analysis (although they seem to oppose one another) and more precisely that these differences cease to exist once we stop trying to exchange the logical notions that Lautréamont proposes in a more or less mocking way for the immediately perceptible meanings. But, if we see in their constancy themes that must in fact reveal something, the meaning of which, behind the apparent meaning, must be put to the test, through a kind of experiment, through the scenes where these themes are presented, it is not then useless to want to know, once again, why Lautréamont, in his fight, chooses God as his adversary, God transformed into a python or a dragon, and not directly the dragon, the python, or the rhinoceros. We cannot thoughtlessly dismiss the logical forms of the book, even if the goal of the book is to move to a far superior discursive level. We are unable to dismiss these forms, because, in a saturated work, there are no pretexts, everything is of equal importance and, in any case, we cannot know ahead of time if these logical forms do not also represent illogical values with an extraordinarily poetic efficiency.[29] We saw in our analysis a resolute machine, a mechanism completely confident about the future of its motion, only making up for what is illegitimate in its method (which separates out the ensemble of the text) through its excesses and the indefinite prolongation of its operation. Beginning from one point of view, analysis must shuffle through the entire work to test it out. When its insufficiency becomes apparent, it must one by one examine all the possible perspectives through which the book will, each time, be entirely and indefinitely interrogated and set back in motion. This is clear, the perpetual movement alone justifies the analysis; once it stops, all of its dangling conclusions, its expected explications, take on a definitive value, and the work, violently separated from itself, breaks apart to make room for a rudimentary infrastructure, clumsily reconstructed from without.

Analysis and the Future of the Work

And yet, the most serious part remains. At fault because of its arbitrary divisions, but making up for these "divisions" by "multiplying" them, analysis sinks to its essential defect. If it wants to compensate for its limits, it needs to expand, in every sense, but in order to pass through the work in every sense, it has to neglect what makes it a creative progression, the irreversible movement of an order of development: whether it be an affirmation within the book that slowly emanates, or the open course of action, not wandering like the vagaries of madness but aspiring toward an end that it brings to light, whether it unveils it for itself and for others, it might only be "understood" in relation to the flow of time. This is precisely what analysis must necessarily disregard, especially if it wants to be as exact as possible, which is to say exhaustive, because, wanting to grasp the book in every possible way, analysis must treat it as a homogenous, immobile zone, like a thing that always existed, its meaning, sought independently of the meaning of its intention, neglecting in particular the movement by which it is made. A major difficulty, that leads to abuses of all kinds. Which reminds us: we undertook the analysis of the theme of cruelty by classifying the cruel images by category: cruelty against

others, against oneself, cruelty of an erotic nature. But—a signifi-
cant omission—this attention to order completely neglected the
order of the book, and the events, taken randomly, have been
arranged together according to their nature, as if this nature by no
means depended on their chronological situation in the work.
Similarly, Bachelard lays out Lautréamont's remarkable bestiary,
but this bestiary puts forward its known facts in the timeless heav-
en of analysis, and each image, assessed and weighed individually,
with painstaking care and limitless attention, is taken from any
part of the book, on which it sheds light through a methodical
comparison with all the others and within a perfect indifference
for the moment that it appears in the composition in this unique
totality called *Maldoror*. As fabricators of analysis, we therefore act
as if, working in a world upset by a cataclysm, it were necessary for
us, in order to piece it back together, to rely on the only objective
characteristics of these fragments, the true order of which had
nothing to do with the disorder born of the randomness of their
dispersion.

It is true that *Maldoror* makes us think precisely about a figure
engendered by the capriciousness of a prodigious catastrophe:
without any apparent unity, it seems to affirm a perpetual rupture,
to which we would only know how to respond by surrendering
ourselves to a fundamental alienation. This, in fact, is obvious.
But this is also why it is very important, for those who want to
attain the "meaning" of such a book, to entrust oneself to the
unfolding of events, in its temporal "meaning." *A work is made
with time*: this certainty, at least, endures.[30] We may or may not
see *Maldoror* as a masterpiece of automatic writing, but in either
case, we are confident that at a certain moment in time
Lautréamont began to write, that at another moment he stopped
writing, and that the duration of his work, this progressive bring-
ing to light of words, in part coincided with the impulse to create,
in other words, with the progression of transformations through
which the work, while being made, was directed toward one
meaning more than another, so that this "meaning" hereafter was
part of the "meaning" of the work and constitutes perhaps the

clearest part of its signification. There is in *Maldoror* an enormous continuity, an enormous discontinuity; everyone senses this. Each stanza is profoundly connected, to such an extent that we easily view it as having been written by a single hand that never stops. And yet, between stanzas, as between cantos, the white of the page that separates them introduces an insurmountable distance, and the mind jumps from one to the next with the anxiety of a walker that truly knows he is forging ahead, who knows that "time is passing," but knows nothing more.

The Central Experience of *Maldoror*

For some years, critics, like Rémy de Gourmont, seemingly best informed on what might be the function of lucidity in the work, acknowledged a complete absence of lucidity in Ducasse.[31] Today, writers, like Roger Caillois, no less informed on the characteristics of a lucid mind, first admire his "clairvoyance," his "insight," his unique strength as an author to not only know what he is saying, but, while saying it, to consider, comment on, and correct himself.[32] Others, while sharing this admiration, justify it with completely opposed reasons. Julien Gracq, for example, sees in *Maldoror* the vengeance of the irrational, the dazzling affirmation of dark forces, the volcanic explosion of subterranean, incandescent layers.[33] Perhaps one must be amazed by a work wherein a lucid reader recognizes at once a contemptible and an admirable absence of lucidity, and a creation that is admirably conscious and admirably foreign to consciousness.

The signs of conscious writing abound in *Maldoror*. There is not one single sentence, as long and as intricate as it might be, that does not direct a visible, reasonable meaning. There is not one stanza wherein the linkage of sentences is not justified logically. The reader in search of straightforward rationality finds everything that is necessary to follow a text, one that corresponds, with all of its meticulous syntactical agreements, with a thought that is perfectly assured of its course. Additionally, it is to be believed that if the mocking tone completely infused an unfolding discord into the "discerning" level of the language, this irony would, however, include, even when it becomes a truly fabulous power, a guarantee of lucidity: mockery that crosses out and renounces the sentence in progress, is therefore conscious of the sentence, assesses all of its nuances, since it corrects them—and if this correction, while picking apart the initial thought, brings with it a dangerous imbalance, irony, highly conscious of such a divergence, seizes upon these digressions, leads them, in a profound way, and reintroduces them into the ensemble as intentionally senseless surprises. Yes, "reason" is astonishingly solid in Lautréamont, no rational reader can doubt this.

But this reason is, justly, so powerful, it is so overarching that it also seems to embrace every foolish impulse and to be able to *understand* the strangest aberrant forces, the subterranean constellations by which it is guided and which it nonetheless carries with it without losing itself or them.

If we see Lautréamont as a writer blinded or enlightened by dark forces alone, we must then attribute the ability to write as much to these unknown forces as to the most thoughtful art. Not only does he who advances in reading *Maldoror* always find, in order to draw on a meaningful intention, the movement leading and coordinated by a meaning that, if it is not yet apparent, is promised, but he meets, midst the rubble of traditional rules, the precautions, the conscientious predictions of a language that undoubtedly knows where it is going, even if it is always saying what it is doing, if it always actualizes what it announces, if, perfectly scornful of disconcerting the reader too easily, it never leaves an unexplained enigma. The composition of *Maldoror* is often shrouded in mystery. It is not uncommon that such development be abruptly interrupted—though without interrupting the continuity of the discourse—giving way to another scene, deprived of any connection with this development. On the theme, "I was looking for a soul that resembled my own and I was unable to find one" (93), one stanza engages a long, methodical search, which it suddenly abandons in order to undertake a story of shipwreck, of ocean, of storm, and this story, having nothing to do with the first part of the stanza, leads us so far and for so long that we have long forgotten from whence we came when, in the final lines, the writer, retying the end to the beginning, permits the common thread, which he has never given away, to appear: "At last I had found someone who resembled me" (99). Many stanzas, behind their disorderly surface, have the same vigilant composition. We do not know where we are going, we lose ourselves in pitiful mazes, but the labyrinth that leads us astray is revealed to have been constructed precisely to lead us astray, and to lead us astray further still, so as to allow us to think we have found ourselves again.

In many of these cases, Lautréamont visibly transports devices of mystery unique to popular fiction and mystery novels into his style. It is his own language that becomes a mysterious plot, an action sequence marvelously united with a detective novel, where the most powerful obscurities are the unforeseen moments, where the *coups de théâtre* are replaced with images, unusual murders by violent acts of sarcasm, and where the guilty party merges with the reader, who is always taken to task. These intentions explode in the sixth book, when Lautréamont says, after Nerval, his rosary of beautiful hermetic phrases, which he clarifies one at a time, though with a bizarre disinterest that seems to want to permit doubt to hover over the nature of these practices, since he only ever grasps a fleeting stability, the future of which does not belong to him.

The Hope of a Mind

It goes without saying that we do not intend to explain all of the mysteries of the composition of *Maldoror*—mysteries of the most disturbing kind—solely by means of the forethought of the author, always more knowledgeable than the reader, more capable of foreseeing an outcome of which the reader is ignorant, and wherein he freely uses this ignorance as the path leading to the outcome. But this, at least, seems certain: *Maldoror*—which would be difficult to praise as the work of a mind absent from itself—assumes within it, at the highest level, all the qualities that Lautréamont justly proclaims for the self: "cold" attention, "implacable logic," "relentless caution," "ravishing clarity" (which multiplies meanings while complicating the labyrinth of its influence); all the qualities he declares he mastered through commerce with "mathematical saints," who were initially "foreign" to him. The solemnity with which he averts us from reason is in fact there to teach us that reason is something foreign to him and that this rationality, for Lautréamont as for everyone, but for him more so than for others, only represents a long, tragic, and obstinate road toward true reason (83 ff.).

The more we multiply the instances of Lautréamont's powerful lucidity, the more the obscurity of this work, the dark force of which is extreme, is able to make us obscure; if we must explain this darkness through the game of "ravishing clarity," if through it alone the impression comes to us that "a nightmare has taken hold of the pen," this clarity will in the end only deepen the mystery. Regardless of whether Lautréamont deliberately made *Maldoror* a stupefying book, it is not because he assures us that we must doubt it. He says so, therefore it is true.[34] But if he tells us this, it is because it is not exactly true; moreover, from the moment that he shamelessly makes clear his intention to surprise us, this surprise cannot be softened by our knowledge of it. It is, on the contrary, linked to our expectations, to its admonition, all the more effective since, hitting us in the light of day, not unexpectedly, it strips us of all hope of ever shielding ourselves from it.

In the final stanza of the book, at a moment when Lautréamont himself, having reached the end, experiences in his way the feeling of someone who no longer needs his path, he announces to his reader that he wanted to "cretinise" him (214). In Lautréamont, rather than the brutality of impudence, the fact that there is still something evasive, ambiguous, and fleeting in such powerful blows, is bizarre. To stun the reader? Perhaps, but how? Stupidity, he says, is not enough, nor is exhaustion; one must also have magnetic power, one must dominate the dream that ends not in stupidity, but in stupor, that is, within the passivity of a consciousness that sees everything and can do nothing.[35] We are reminded that hypnotism was very much in vogue at the time. But the important thing is not that Lautréamont might have had the idea to transform language and literature into a powerful enterprise of magnetic numbing—the idea of associating poetry and magnetism is present in Baudelaire and Poe—though it shows, within its design, a boldness that will not be surpassed even by Surrealism, drunk by the magnetic sun. In this affirmation wherein the reader discovers himself suddenly under the power of a gaze, the firm lucidity of which is going to obscure his own, there is something more astonishing, more troubling than an allusion to a new literary resource. We see ourselves in it soon enough: the situation in which he claims to push his reader is the same situation as that in which Maldoror is engaged. The reader of *Maldoror* recognizes, as one of its pervasive themes, the fear, the threat of sleep: a strange sleep, which Maldoror refuses, against which he fights with "a remarkable fervor," but which is incessantly able to carry him off because within the refusal to sleep, sleep already exists; in insomnia, it triumphs. The motif of "I am not sleeping, I am never sleeping," if it plagues the whole of the book, specifically makes itself heard in the stanza about sleep and in the last stanza of Canto V (the stanza about the spider and the immense sucking).[36] Across these pages one sees how Maldoror, fallen into a kind of magnetic trap, is in the grip, not of any old nightmare, but of the central tragedy of day and night, that of lucidity struggling against itself, against becoming something else. Lucid Maldoror shows that he is, that he wants to be *at any price*, and to be of a lucidity that never recants; but sometimes this too powerful lucidity is blinded, becomes the haggard heaviness of a sleepless night, sometimes, surprised by sleep (or sometimes by death or even madness), it continues, an "eye that never shuts," at the heart of the decomposition of eternity, at the depth of an empty head, behind a dead mind, in the "cadaverous reason" it perseveres, it is reconstituted, always newly present in the absence that pushed it away.

Without entering into an examination of this description, we see what is at stake. First, an incessantly affirmed resolution to always see clearly; thereafter the cloudy, tormented feeling, precisely recognized by the trap that is at the base of this lucidity, because through the continual distancing of sleep, it welcomes a more tragic sleep, it becomes that sleep, a prisoner of the conditioning at the heart of which it resides. Lautréamont thinks that clairvoyance triumphs in the end, but he knows and he discovers the strange struggle this victory announces and through whose transformations lucidity must seek itself, since the "enchantment" that paralyzes lucidity at precisely the possibility, which it finds dreadful—of dying without dying—which reveals it to be present in the most somber moments of the night.

From these singular pages, we only need, for the moment, to keep this in mind: that, between lucidity and obscurity, in the experience of Maldoror all kinds of relationships exist, disturbing and even tragic relationships, hostility-based harmony, hostile complicity; victory that is failure. And, at the same time, these pages confirm that, even in this nocturnal density, where day seems to be lost light, Lautréamont, continuing his persistent struggle, never made a pact with darkness: he has one solitary concern "not to succumb," "to get out of this bed," "a more difficult problem than one might think" (169). In recalling such a situation, we will judge it less strange that *Maldoror*, precisely where this situation appears, might simultaneously testify to its author's powerful consciousness and to sink deeper and deeper into dark regions where pointless passion prevails through wild instinct. Lucidity pervades every part of the book, it drives it, composes it. But the work—lucid par excellence, in the sense that lucidity is its principal recourse, as well as being that which is at stake—because of this lucidity overflows with clarity throughout and affirms it, seeks it, loses it, then finds it and finally denounces it.

Perhaps this is not very mysterious. We are now used to the fact that words like lucidity, consciousness, and reason do not correspond to one simple usage, that lucidity can be present and absent, that it sometimes disappears while continuing to watch over the work, that it looks out from behind distraction, that it acts passively, like Lynceus who keeps watch, not from the top of a tower, but while at work in subterranean depths. And we are now used to the fact that the most conscious writer, insofar as the book that he composes brings a profound part of him into play, by no means dismisses the powers of his mind, but, on the contrary, summons them into association with this book and asks the book to help and deepen these powers. Between his work and his lucidity, he establishes an impulse to compose and to develop, mutually, an extremely difficult task, important and complex, a task that we call *experience*, at the end of which the book will not only use the mind but will have been used by it, in such a way that the book can be said to be absolutely lucid, if *it is the work of lucidity* and if *lucidity is its work*.

We will not hesitate to say that *Maldoror* appears to be the most remarkable example of this type of work, a model of this kind of literature that does not entail a model, more striking, because of its scope and its developments (because duration is essential in this enterprise), than Rimbaud's *Illuminations*—too powerful, in a certain way, for the mind, the *Illuminations* leave the mind with nothing but the memory of a dazzling experience—and *A Season in Hell*, which, rather than being an experience, is the *récit* of an experience.[37] This is why it seems so important to read *Maldoror* as a progressive creation, created in time and with time, a "work in progress" which Lautréamont undoubtedly drives where he wants, but which also drives him into the unknown, about which he says "Let's follow the current that drags us along" not because he lets himself be dragged along, drifting with ferocious and blind forces, but because the "sweeping" force of the work is its way of being ahead of itself, of preceding itself, the future even of its lucidity in the process of transformation.

What did Lautréamont have on his mind the night that he scribbled the first words: "May it please the heaven that . . . " (27)? It is not enough to say that, in this initial moment, Lautréamont had not completely formed the memory of the six cantos that he was going to write. We have to say more: not only were the six cantos not in his mind, but this mind did not exist yet; the only goal that he could have was that distant mind, that hope of a mind that, at the moment when *Maldoror* would be written, would lend him all the strength he would need to write it.

It is no doubt admirable that, as a completed work, *Maldoror* presents itself as a totality without cracks, like the basaltic block on which Maldoror sadly recognizes the solidity of his own existence, drawn from all dissolutions. Is there another work like this one, on the one hand completely at the mercy of time, inventing or discovering its meaning while it is being written, an accomplice closely linked to its duration, that remains meanwhile a mass without a beginning or an end, a timeless substance, a simultaneity of words, wherein every trace, before and after, seems to have been erased, and forever forgotten? Therein lies one of the great surprises of this book, but one that we must, for the moment, try to avoid. Rather, that we might glimpse Lautréamont himself, perhaps we should look for him at the moment when, with no one there, on the fifth floor in an empty room, lit by a single candle flicking on the white page, one hand, ah, certainly one very beautiful hand, forms itself in solitude to write, "May it please heaven that ... ," and to write in response to these five words.[38]

The First Canto: Dazet

Lautréamont placed a categorical break between the first five cantos and the sixth. The difference between these two parts is, in fact, striking. We also know that the circumstances of publication also placed a break between the first canto and the other five, the first canto having been published alone (in August 1868 and without the author's name attached), whereas the entire work, as we know it, appeared under the name of the Comte de Lautréamont the following year (before October 1869), though, thanks to the police, it was never offered for sale. These circumstances may seem unimportant, and in fact they hardly are, but they seem to impart a sign to us. First, we can conclude from this initial publication that, at the time it was arranged, only the first canto of *Maldoror* had been written. This is at least very probable. The first canto does not form more of a totality than those that follow it. Since Ducasse then seems so curious to be published, he might just as well have had the first two cantos appear together, or more, if he had written more. But he had as of yet only written this one. The hand that scribbled "May it please heaven that . .·. " has therefore scribbled only the fifty-two pages that would be set on the Balitout printer's plate, then mysteriously the hand stopped. Why? For how long? Who could say? When it once again began to write, there is reason to believe that the first canto was being readied for print, even that it had already appeared, already drifted into silence, this because, beginning canto II, what does this hand write? Precisely those words that evoke the uncertainties of an uncertain publication: "What became of Maldoror's first canto since his mouth, filled with leaves of belladonna, let it slip in a moment of meditation across the kingdoms of wrath? What happened to that canto? ... We do not precisely know" (59).[39] In fact, this can only be either an allusion or a prophecy.

We also know that between the first edition of the first canto and the text of this canto as it was revealed in the text as a whole, several formal changes appeared. Some were minor corrections.[40] With the exception, however, of one: so impressive it is, in a sense so unexpected, that, without exaggerating its revelatory impact— and since it distracts our eyes from a spectacle that we do not have the right to see—one generally prefers not to linger on this point too long. The change is the following: in all the passages where, in the definitive edition, the strangest of the animal figures come into play, either through invocations or through their presence in the "story"—the *octopus of the silkenglance,* the *rhinolophus whose snout is topped by a horseshoe-shaped crest,* the *venerable louse,* the *toad* in the final stanza, and, finally, the *acarus sarcoptes that causes crabs* in the last sentence—the text of the previous version interjects, in these places, the name Dazet (Georges Dazet was a fellow student at the Lycée de Tarbes with Ducasse; his name also appears in the dedications of the *Poésies;* he died, we are told, in 1919).

This Dazet is a surprise. It is like a slice of reality introduced into the most unreal book that we possess; a little fragment of the historical Ducasse visibly incorporated (there are others, but they can only be suspected) into the myth of Lautréamont.[41] When he begins the first canto, we see that the emerging author of *Maldoror* still knows the name of Dazet, that he wants not only to associate it with his work, but to have it play a rather amicable role, that of a friendship that has already weathered storms and is naturally very ambiguous. In other words, the *unchanged* name and face of Dazet penetrate into the ideal mind of Lautréamont.

It seems that some critics were privately bothered, not by this memory but by the deletion behind the extraordinary, untranslatable image of the *octopus of the silkenglance*, which revealed that there was something, and what? A kind classmate from school. The critics uncomfortably concluded that the sublime hand was, after all, driven like any other banal hand, by an author, who was happy to, we know, give pretty names to pretty nothings or strange names to the most ordinary things. What then is there, definitively, behind all this unnerving language, behind these scenes, these figures, wherein we think we see the world change? What is going on in the mind from which this language follows? Sadly, nothing more than a little Dazet.

Possibly. But this does not offend us. We would only be half surprised if someone from long ago suddenly came to us to testify: "But then what are you looking for? 'Rhinolophus,' 'acarus sarcopte,' insignificant nicknames from school; 'rhinoceros' (which is God, as we know, in canto VI), is Mr. Hinstin's nickname, the professor of rhetoric." This would not be of any greater interest, even less, in fact, than the references to *Revelations* or to Baudelaire. As far as words go, the rhinolophus and the *fulgore* lantern holder certainly had to come from somewhere: if they came from a natural history book, from nocturnal rumination, or from an adolescent joke, it hardly matters, the important thing is not knowing the fortuitous origin of the words and images used by Isidore Ducasse, but grasping how these random words became the first words, and found a new and primary origin in the still nonexistent Lautréamont to whom they simultaneously give birth. Far from recognizing the word "octopus" used in place of Dazet as a flagrant offense to literary artifice, we see therein proof that *Maldoror* was not a work without consequences for its author, that it revealed a number of things to him, that it changed him, transformed him, and that, through this experience, Dazet having ceased being Dazet, in his stead, beneath his appearance, emerged, from the depths, *the octopus of the silkenglance.*

The unity of the Cantos—at least of the first five of them—seems very strong, to such an extent that from beginning to end we sometimes have the feeling of an immobile vertigo, as if nothing was ever going to change. Therein, however, lies only one aspect of the truth. With a little mindfulness, we notice, to the contrary, through the course of the book, while it progresses, an undetectable but constant and deep transformation. Even the "atmosphere" becomes something other, even the language, even the irony. It is only in canto IV that the long, misleading discourses begin, the run-on sentences, the infinite twists and turns that, in search of their own divergence, suddenly freeze in a black immensity; the remaining straightforward images then become unbelievable;[42] the irony that until then was satisfied to skim the surface of the work, through a counter-meaning, the meaning of a word, skims over itself, exalts in the whirlwind of negating figures through which the most glorious affirmations slip. The air that we breathe is no longer the same: it is an air of such an extreme animal density that the metamorphoses, which were so rare and, in the beginning, more sketched than realized, are accomplished in the open while exposing the depth, impossible to see, of their substance.

If we read only the first canto, and as it first appeared—a legitimate reading, since Ducasse hoped for it—we must say that, while the literary meaning of these pages remains extremely powerful, and although some of the famous elements of the book are found therein, we do not yet see the transformative power in action, the power that, at a certain moment, will change these admirable words, these burlesque scenes, and these stupefying images into a world before the world, fabulous darkness, inscribed into language, an immense existence returned to its origins. The first canto is not quite this. It would naturally be impossible to imagine, from this text, the project that Ducasse has in mind, if he has one. But we can comment on it. First, at this moment in the work, the story of Maldoror the vampire is more clear and more stable than in any other section. This Maldoror visibly follows every kind of accursed character that macabre literature placed within the grasp of the imagination. He plays his Byronic role with a conviction that is, for the most part, literary. The temptation scene, while composed according to the tranquil rules of art, is only a singular version of Goethe's "Erlkönig" (44–49).[43] The gravedigger's scene is odd, because Hamlet, having become a vampire after writing on skulls, also wants to sleep in the graves (49–54). The mysterious Luciferian dialogue between Maldoror, fallen archangel, and the toad that implores him to remember his origin, is, in the first version, a straightforward dialogue between two former classmates; the toad, at this particular moment, is only Dazet, and Dazet, more than the representative of God, appears to be a sincere, well-intentioned friend, who does not share in his companion's ideas, scolds him for his bad behavior, is frightened by the strangeness of his sick mind, and who, also, would like to be loved more.[44] Meanwhile, the dialogue and the canto end with these troubling words from Dazet: "Farewell, then, don't hope to find Dazet again on your journey. He is going to die with the knowledge that you did not love him. Why am I counted among existences, if Maldoror does not think about me! You will see a procession pass by this road that no one accompanies; you say: 'It's him!' You have been the cause of my death." The truth is that at this moment Dazet effectively dies, and dies so completely that the hand that pushed him into nothingness will later return to the past to erase every trace of his existence.

Between Ducasse and Lautréamont

It is undeniable that this first canto is closer than the others to the literature of its era, more submissive to literary influences, that Baudelaire visibly appears therein, as do Dante and Byron and Goethe and Sue and Shakespeare. Marcel Jean and Arpad Mezei, who have both sought to reconstruct Lautréamont's "project," think that, in this first book, where the prenatal life of man and of the world would be sketched out, Ducasse has intentionally inspected the masterpieces of humanity, which he has deposited in each stanza like a figurative transposition. For example, say these critics, stanza VIII (pgs. 34–37), wherein dogs howl and fight each other in the grip of some sort of rage, is the *Illiad*; stanza IX (pgs. 37–43), the stanza on the ocean, is the *Odyssey*.[45] Naturally, this is possible, but we are not convinced, first because such a plan, abstract, methodical, authorial, seems from the outset intolerable, in advance, to creative force. We are sure that the phantom of Lautréamont would have reduced Isidore Ducasse to silence, if he had expected to impose such a plan on him; or, in other words, Lautréamont would have remained eternally on the other side of the white page, this sheet of paper tacked to the wall, silently fluttering in the heat of the candle, such that, through the quiet rustling, Ducasse, "the young man who yearns for glory," could still hear the unborn names Maldoror and Lautréamont.

If allusions to masterworks are visible in the first canto, it is simply that this canto is the first, that the work has yet to do its work, such that "the young man that yearns for glory" is still very close to the glory of others.[46] He only has a slight inkling of what he must become, at the heart of a creation that will create him so that he can create it. It is therefore remarkable that this first text, when it appeared, appeared without a name: behind it, no one, no author; because Lautréamont still does not exist, and Ducasse, already, is dying (like Dazet).[47] Everyone who writes will recognize the agonizing strangeness of this solemn moment—not anguish before the work to be done, but before the being to become, the being that one would know how to be only by means of a long, persevering, and exalting movement in the void, during which this being that jumped will no longer be someone, but be the jump. Our impression is that Ducasse jumped off from a rather simple project, inspired by the literary concerns of his day, by a theoretically vague reverie on Evil and the absurd vicissitudes of Existence, a reverie that, in order to be sustained, chooses a framework within the grasp of every young imagination—but dangerously undefined—that of the Accursed One, alternately a vampire, a fallen angel, a black man cut off from the community, in every way an ambiguous power that torments others because of the torment it withstands.

Now, if we return to the first book and if we inspect it, to know what is already there, what is not yet there, we are led to different considerations. Compared to the cantos of "maturity," it undoubtedly stands out due to its literary seriousness. Long sections form ordered and studied compositions that resemble prose poems (we know that *Gaspard de la Nuit* was found at Montevideo, in Ducasse's father's library; Baudelaire's *Petit poèmes en prose* began to appear in 1862; *Paroles d'un Croyant* in 1834[48]). The stanza on the dogs in the moonlight visibly aspires to poetic effect. Even the great, "serious and cold" stanza on the ocean is spurred on by an ideal of lyrical eloquence, by a concern for "beautiful" language that irony does not alter. This preoccupation will not disappear with the first canto. In canto II, the narratives are no less writerly, nor the literary ambitions less present, and such concern persists throughout the entire work. A certain linguistic premeditation, resources of a balanced composition, musical arrangements are found throughout; the meticulously calculated refrains confirm them. Sometimes, Lautréamont deliberately constructs disorder with order, as in the Falmer stanza in which, following the process Baudelaire used in *Harmonie du Soir* ("Evening Harmony"), the language unravels and comes together again in a movement similar to the cycle of the eternal return (156–58). All this confirms the skill of Ducasse's writing. Except that it appears as if, at the beginning, the literary precautions do not aim toward much more than the creation of a beautiful work; later, and proportionately as the world opens up, these precautions are going to take the mind further than it knows how to go, these precautions will help it, thanks to the certainty of a concerted language, to persevere in the void, to lose itself and to seize itself anew.

"Toward the Unknown"

Assuredly, in this first canto, we may be struck by the lack of irony, by the absence of metamorphoses, by the very weak hints of animal life and, alternatively, by the almost too serious account of the moral strangeness of the world, an account that, in this general form, will not be repeated again.[49] But, if we can forget the *Maldoror* of what follows and think only about the reigning literature, what strikes us is the irony and the sound, unheard, of this irony: this harsh, cold, cutting of the words, exactly like a razor across a face, this cutting decision that already affirms itself and, if it has not yet inverted language, turns it into a blade so sharp that, by whatever side one grasps it, it cuts, it cleaves.[50] What strikes us, already, by means of comparison or allegory, is the approach of animal realities. The shark is there, from the second stanza, "like the shark in the dark fine air" (28). And, from the first, the whirlwind of cranes that will later impose the law of its movement on the entire work, is foreshadowed in the straight flight of the chilly cranes.[51] From the eighth, Maldoror meets his first "female shark," a strange meeting, because, in the following canto, he is going to mate with this female, though actually he would like to become her son: "If it had been up to *me*, I'd far rather have been the son of a female shark, whose hunger is the friend of tempests, and of the tiger, whose cruelty is well-known: I would not be so wicked" (36). A banal metaphor? True, but justifiably so; at this moment when we are, in fact, within the calm component of the metaphorical intelligence, a more serious phenomenon is produced. The metaphor explodes and, without any other priming, as if something was then seized by Isidore Ducasse, the first signs of a bizarre change appear in him, a change that petrifies him while linking him with subterranean depths: "No one has yet seen the green fissures on my forehead; nor the bones protruding from my spare features, akin to the spiky fins of some huge fish, or to the rocks that cover the seashore" (36). No doubt the "akin to"'s preserve the contact with ordinary reason; the ties are not yet broken. But let's continue to read: at present, Maldoror, crouched down then standing at the bottom of a cavern (where he hides because of his ugliness), is described as turning his head slowly from right to left, from left to right, "for hours on end" (37). Why this strange behavior? And why does it come to the fore precisely at this moment? If we try to approach this strange passivity, feeling the extent to which time is slowed by it, perhaps we will sense what kind of profound inertia is beginning to immobilize Maldoror, at the heart of a space wherein his actions come apart. Where is he going? We do not know. But if such a change in "time" might have something to do with the seed of the dangerous changes in the metaphor "akin to," this is what we foresee: the image opened up a breach in Maldoror's human life span; something begged to happen. What? Hastily, the experience concludes and the violent blow that strikes him on the head throws him back into the world.

What is, at this moment, so impressive for the reader who knows what is going to happen, is that Ducasse is in danger and he does not see it. He is surrounded by banal figures of rhetoric, he summons dogs, the glowworm, the raven, the immortal pelican, the viper, the toad, the whale, the hammer, the deformed fish, and everything is there under the reassuring pretext of moral analogy.[52] He however appears not to know that they only came so quickly because summoned by a force stronger than he is; they are a temptation, the fear of a possibility, not yet identified and lost in the depths of a still impenetrable past. From the beginning, it is this impulse that several stanzas would let us glimpse, more than anything else, the great praise of the ocean. No doubt a similar hymn, returning glory to the infinitude of the waters, dominates the entire canto. Through this celebration, the book affirms its accord with the underwater depths, proclaims their sovereignty over it and its sovereignty over these depths; it knows that its path will pass by this "kingdom of viscosity" and that this abyss will be its abyss. The mythic riches of the ocean being inexhaustible, every image can find its origin therein. Marcel Jean and Arpad Mezei tell us that the ocean is the unconscious and that the hymn is to its glory. Very well. H. R. Linder tells us that the ocean is the image of lost identity, of a paradisial Unity for which the lacerations of this world, the cruel struggle of good and evil, make Lautréamont nostalgic. Why not? Lautréamont does not make a mystery of it: "Old ocean, you are the symbol of the identity: always equal unto yourself"(38). And this unity, this "elementary" geometry, pleases him like what he found metaphorically satisfying in the demands of a reason thirsty for exactitude. It is true, too, that the ocean—the waves of which are crystalline, while the depths are impenetrable—the ocean truly represents Maldoror's unique lucidity, if his lucidity is such that clarity added to clarity produces therein, and spreads, the blackest shadows. But what is the importance of these little bursts of meaning? Lautréamont carefully informs us: here, there are no limits, "A formidable maw. It must be vast toward the bottom, in the direction of the unknown!" (41). It is therefore this direction that it designates for us and, at precisely this moment, he himself enters therein. Up to this point, in this stanza, the paragraphs follow one another in an orderly fashion and with a controlled calmness. But the *unknown* suddenly passes into Maldoror's voice and a name, like the revelation of the primordial ocean, reveals to Ducasse what he had not yet seen: the "old ocean, great celibate" breaks with all the preceding classic figures. All of a sudden, for the first time, appears the "dark mystery" of a taciturn virility, of an almighty solitude that would search in vain for the consolation of the couple, a kind of solitary Father that he compares "to the vengeance of God,"[53] but which is no more the image of God than God is the image of the father, if in these figures we expect to introduce distinct and precise categories. The important thing is not in the meaning of such a power, because obviously this power does not and cannot have a fixed and clear meaning. What matters is the movement that carries Lautréamont toward it and pushes him to propose an alliance with it: "Answer me, Ocean, do you want to be my brother?" (42). And immediately, as with all declarations of fraternity (and, especially, with purely erotic impulses), he will happen upon the possibility that the perspective of such a union opens up; a trembling, a furor, and a transformative violence respond, in such a way that the ocean becomes the anger of the ocean, the image of unleashed energy, of this madness in the course of which, for Maldoror, feelings change signs, love becomes hate, hate friendship, remorse already begins, and the symptoms of a possible metamorphosis appear. For, we see, it is initially only a question of one single figure: the claws of the ocean. What could be more classic?[54] But these claws take and find shape, and the dragon of stanza XXXIII (117 ff.) is already sketched, here receiving the guarantee of his elementary origin and of his "magnificent" nature. At this moment, Ducasse's always magnificently regulated sentence structure is, in reality, prey to the most contradictory movements: the ocean is "hideous," this "ugliness" that, we know full well, is Maldoror's particularity and obsession. However, the ocean, with its formidable majesty (at the heart of which remorse can be heard), throws Lautréamont into admiration and love. Then—and almost as soon—in a completely contrary sentiment, because such majesty, being admirable, evokes so fiercely, in contrast, the baseness of men: "I cannot love you, I loathe you" (42). But hate in turn is too great; it, too, immediately becomes friendship, and even more: confidential passion, desire, a thirst for intimacy. "Your secret destiny I know not: all that concerns you interests me . . . So tell me . . . Tell me everything . . . Tell me (me alone)" (42).

All these movements may appear to analysis as at once highly explicable and of mediocre meaning, which the informality of irony would diminish once again. And, in fact, here it is hardly a question of psychology or ontology; the commentators have been busy trying to show that, in the end, if Maldoror does reject the ocean, it is because, although it is Unity, unity itself being only the opposite of diversity, it is already accounted for within the dialectic of the multiple and would not be able to satisfy his desire for union (here we see which exegesis we might follow). But who feels that the interest lies elsewhere? Who sees the tension that violence places on his language and on his being, a violence so powerful that it does not permit any respite in the excessiveness of one single passion and that this instability, which forces it to go beyond the form of feelings, is able to bring it beyond every form? Who also has the premonition of the kind of vertigo through which Maldoror enters into contact with this indeterminate power that is the ocean, the primordial center of metamorphoses, an originally pure element, an originally vague, diffused substance, formless and ready to take on any form, an existence as compact as rock, but living, a fullness always one and always other, and wherein he who enters becomes an other. In this stanza, there is, in fact, an immense transference from Maldoror to the ocean, between both figures an indecision, and we do not know any more than confusedly to whom this hideousness belongs—to whom the anger, to whom the remorse—as if Lautréamont, to maintain his equilibrium, had to unload onto another his violent excesses, so that the ocean sketches the beginnings of personification, while at the same time Maldoror sees himself lose his person, which he is trying to grasp within infinity personified.

The Gravitation of Themes, the Pulverization of Images

We have imagined that Ducasse set out from a rather simple design. What is always outside the point of departure lets itself be recognized in various ways: through the nearly abstract form within which the theme of evil is still present; through the role played by the Maldoror vampire storyline; through the influence exerted by popular literary works of the day, which act, if not as models, at least as stimulants. That, from the beginning, this design is something other than literary, and that, behind the masterpiece about to be written—a traditional, adolescent dream—Ducasse senses an obligation, a duty, an experience to suffer through, this is obvious. Maldoror is not just any Accursed One, he is the *Montevideen*, and it is precisely in these pages that the connection between the two people is explicitly confirmed. It does not follow that the hero of *Maldoror* renounces every mythical existence: sometimes Maldoror is simply a human "I," as close as possible to Ducasse's personal history (as we might suspect it to be); sometimes he is truly a mythical character. But this shift to myth does not distance him from his author and, in many cases, the opposite is true. We see in this new dimension and in this accession into mythic time one of the forms of Lautréamont's experience: either, through distancing himself, he is forced to see himself in the strangest light, or, through this bias, the shift makes bearable the disclosure of a reality that would otherwise expose him to too great dangers.

The romantic theme of evil is certainly a literary theme, and perhaps Ducasse believes he chose it for this reason alone. But if he is deceived on this point, or if he is mistaken, even more naively, in imagining that, through his book, he is going to advance "the problem of evil,"[55] how would he not at the same time know that "evil" is for him not simply an abstract category, but that this word must also hide a more personal truth, a hypnotizing mystery, shrouded in his past, toward which he is carried by the desire, itself obscure, to draw everything into the light? In fact, what is remarkable from the very beginning of *Maldoror* is the movement, at once obstinate and infinitely cautious, that accomplishes, stanza by stanza, the engagement, the approach, the uncovering of a certain number of hidden things, a movement that gives the book its strange and admirable composition. We know that in canto V, Lautréamont's lucidity has "explained" exactly, by describing the flight of the starlings, the oddities of this composition (159–60), how it responds to the complex formula of whirlwinds, that follow two proclivities at once: a tendency to return to the center—in other words, to be concentrated around the point where the passage from the most sweeping movement to a state of rest is about to take place—and a projective tendency, a result of the displacement from the center by the same forces that seek, that desire this center, and yet, almost at the limit, reject it ad infinitum. This description has always inspired the admiration of experts: of psychoanalysts, who see therein a figure of cyclic obsession; of Marcel Jean and Arpad Mezei, who discover herein a general principle of explication, that of convergence-divergence, and point out its scientific value.[56] It is, in fact, hard not to be amazed, when one sees this adolescent offer the most satisfying elucidation from the most obscure side of his work (obscure, because it eludes the clarity of traditional forms and also because the most somber elements of himself are at work herein), where purely poetic lucidity is unified with purely rational lucidity. It is in fact at this moment that one feels bound to link reason and madness, clarity and opacity, within him. We should not, however, forget that the image of the starlings only appears in canto V, at the moment when experience itself shifts so visibly from the center that it is enough for Ducasse to simply observe the evolution of his work to decipher its meaning and, thanks to the lucidity of his thought, to grant this meaning the ideal precision of a formula.

If each stanza is developed according to an order wherein art is occasionally visible, the ensemble of the stanzas does not follow an apparent order but instead apparently follows an inclination toward disorder and discontinuity. It is clear, from the start, that Ducasse meant to cut his book, to divide it up into fragments that were to be separated by insurmountable intervals. Why this regulated breaking, this ever new point of departure, which he seems to want to impose on himself each time? For the shock value (as he says in canto VI)? A requirement imposed by the very division of the text into stanzas in order to arrive at a series of rather short prose poems? Possibly. But the arrangement into stanzas does not prevent him from constructing, when he so chooses (in the last canto), a short text simultaneously free and possessed of a very sufficient, logical coherence, exactly the same kind of composition that appears in the interior organization of each stanza. As for surprising the reader, this preoccupation did, in fact, please Ducasse, but it pleased him for a reason which he soon saw: the reader is him and what he must surprise is the tormented center of himself, in flight toward the unknown.

To make Lautréamont say more than he says, to give an expression to our mode of what he has himself put into words, is perhaps not a fitting method. But the temptation is strong. Because, reading *Maldoror*, one feels a very obscure nudge from without to within, an alternation riddled with apparitions and disappearances, with impulses of both attraction and repulsion, such a complex system of eclipsing and brightening stars that no reader is able, at any particular moment, to resist the desire to hasten such an elucidation, nor to get his impatient hands on the "reality" that has yet to emerge. Hence, so many of the interpretations, which we ourselves are making, are but intermediaries, upsurges of meaning, destined to direct us toward the sole term that we might dream of attaining, because it does not exist for us.

There is undoubtedly no book wherein, so obstinately, the situations, the "scenes," the themes, the images, are all repeated, everything always returning to the surface, then going back into the depths, then emerging once more, and once again pulling away. One thinks of a kind of planetary gravitation that, through extremely complex rules, would impose, at precisely calculated periodic moments, the return of all these corpuscles before our eyes, for the short instant when they come together and form a visible ensemble, before breaking apart in order to complete the nocturnal part of their trajectory. But this figure is still less exact than that of the "whirlwinds," which is itself, definitively speaking, hardly exact. Because these corpuscles, if they do reappear with a potentially calculable regularity, reappear otherwise than they were: they have often gone through a radical transformation, it is like they exploded en route or borrowed from their passing associations with other new possibilities of character and figure. We said that everything repeats itself, but neither is anything repeated, and the themes, the situations undergo, through the movement that assures their return, a change that prevents their return: what returns is another situation and another theme that we do not recognize. It would, certainly, hardly be exact to compare these phenomena to the calculated enchantments of a musical composition: first, because, as both literature and poetry are not music, these analogies are always improper and generally satiate us with an illusion; moreover, if it so happens that we are able to isolate within language its pure musical essence and to imagine, from this essence, particular combinations that can be said to be proper to music, nothing like this takes place in *Maldoror*, wherein the returns, repetitions, and transformed identities follow entirely different necessities and imply an ever more intense tension between the almighty lucidity of the outside and the treacherous lucidity of within, which, a prisoner of itself, is also an accomplice of its prison.

As much as the repetitions of language—the "I hail you, Old Ocean"—and of form appear concerted to us, the repetitions of motifs and of images seem to elude every deliberate decision and to rise again from a much more obscure zone, from this trick of consciousness that at once sees and does not see, knows and does not know. A good example of this is found in the stanza that follows the hymn to the ocean. This stanza is loosely attached to the preceding one through these words: "I want to die, cradled on the waves of the stormy sea" (43). But this "I want to die" is rather unique. In a certain way it tears apart time, so that, through this tear, Maldoror sees himself already in his funeral chamber and actually laid out on his deathbed, finding thereby the possibility of existence on the other side of death and of extracting a present life from the event that definitively renders this life past. This situation is natural enough here because it corresponds to that of the vampire (who is a dead man in whom death lives), and this precise situation once again launches us into the story of Maldoror as vampire, a progression that carries us through to two sentences from the end. There, everything changes. Maldoror, "awoken" by the rhinolophus—Dazet in the first version—seeing himself still alive, should conclude that all this was nothing but a dream, yet the irony, through a sarcastic concern for coherence or for a more serious reason, only substitutes the idea of a "passing illness" for death, and the stanza concludes with an enigmatic detail that reconciles precisely the idea of a dream with that of sickness: it is that the rhinolophus has taken advantage of sleep in order to suck his blood.[57] This is already a telling episode, since, however peculiar a vampire Maldoror may be, he has his own blood sucked, seemingly to his great satisfaction ("why is this hypothesis not reality!" [44]).

If we now skip to the beginning of canto II, stanza XVI, we attend to a quite different scene. Ducasse has begun working again. Yet he is unable to write: his "pen remains inert" (61). A storm breaks, a bolt of lightning comes to cut in two, in the face, Maldoror, who in this very moment substitutes himself for Ducasse abruptly vaporized. A wonderful wound. Blood gushes forth; a dog laps up "this blood that is getting all over the carpet;" the dog displays even more zeal: "Enough, you greedy dog, enough! . . . your belly's full" (62). As for Maldoror, who has lost a lot of blood, his forehead resting against the ground, what is becoming of him? He is completely healed: his wound is not much more than a scar, a fiendish scar that becomes a distant allusion to "a torment already lost . . . in the night of bygone times" (62). His friend Leman, whose presence we still perceive, is invited to tidy up, while Ducasse begins writing in blood, his fragile wound suddenly reopening. The analogy of the two scenes is evident. In both, troubled time assures Maldoror of the possibility of entering into situations and of escaping them, of living the present moment as if this present was perpetually behind him (because undoubtedly what is at stake is "the night of bygone times"), of being simultaneously dead, sick, and healed. Moreover, the motif of the vampirization, sketched in a brutally direct manner with a few words in canto I, is developed more extensively in the new scene, through detours that conceal it: the dog drinks the blood, just as the rhinolophus sucks it, but the blood, which is really Maldoror's, has already become foreign to him—which does not prevent the procedure from being shown as both desirable and, in the long run, strangely painful. It is clear that the rhinolophus (which Dazet was behind earlier) has now been split in two and is perpetuated in both the dog and Leman, this friend who would function equally well as a housekeeper and a wife. Later, a similar splitting in two will transpire, in such a way that the erotic meaning will be fiercely paraded about: in the course of the scene wherein we see Maldoror aided, in a rape, by an "angry" bulldog (114–15). All these very strange details depend on something else, to which they are linked and that is still more noteworthy: the impossibility of writing, which strikes Ducasse and which dominates the entire scene. A meaningful paralysis that will reappear in many forms in each canto, up to the final scene of Canto V when it is denounced: a paralysis that is itself the paralysis of an "enchantment," of interior lucidity, linked by what it knows and refuses to say. Obviously, Ducasse is alluding to a veritable refusal to speak, the power of which he experiences within himself, a refusal that is the igniting force of his book, the principle of his "work," which he can only overcome through tricks and by apparently giving in to this passivity. How does he overcome this impotence here? In a remarkable way: by attributing the responsibility for its existence to an external force, a divine commandment, to which it is perhaps associated, but which most assuredly offers the advantage of making his struggle possible for him. One can struggle with God, strong as he may be.[58] This is why even the lightning that pulverizes Ducasse and the wound that annihilates Maldoror represents, in reality, a form of rescue, and is already a recovery, because, through this "evil" projected outside of it, the soul begins to penetrate its own evil and to make "the frontiers of madness and those frenzied thoughts that kill slowly" recede— precisely described as such in the same stanza.[59]

Fear is one of the rarest sentiments in *Maldoror*. The two dominant dispositions are an extremely forceful fury and an extremely lethargic passivity; contrary movements that, however, do not oppose one another. If fury implicates the desire for combat and the will to liberate oneself, this desire is "furious;" in other words, it is not only a struggle against evil or "madness," but also evil and madness themselves becoming means, passions for struggle. And likewise, passivity and lethargy do not represent pure and simple abandonment to magnetizing powers; they are still a silent way of struggling, a patient ruse, an ultimate possibility for rebellion and clairvoyance. These nuances must be present in our mind if we want to appreciate the role of intention or the bit of calculation that is revealed, in Ducasse, through the disappearance and reappearance of themes and the pulverization of motifs. The mixture of interminable precaution and revelatory brutality through which, at every moment, he shows an endless groping around something that does not appear, the digressions through which he seems to want to attenuate truth in order to better take it by surprise (and the ostentatious domestic violations, the authoritative voice that he assumes in order to yell secret things at heaven, intending to provoke), are two cunning faces of the same struggle for the light. And, when he seems to have said everything, as in those vociferations wherein his taste for adolescents and his horror of women pass, such an excess of sincerity can also count as a victory of dissimulation, because these dreaded things are no less hidden when affirmed exaggeratedly than when denied. On the contrary, in scenes wherein the errance of language appears to screen his lucidity, it is then perhaps closest to what it is seeking, because, beneath this strangeness of images and of words, it senses itself become other and prepares for its metamorphosis.

In a general way, it is the prudence, the ruses of Lautréamont that are particularly shocking. Although he may be tempted by the worst, we have the feeling that, in moments of greatest verbal madness, wherein everything leads to the fear that a premature revelation, provoked by these very indiscretions of language, forever silences him, he always knows not only what should be said, but what he still must ignore. The division into apparently disconnected stanzas, in this respect, is a great resource. Feigning to always pick up again at the beginning, he is not obligated to again take up his developed themes, nor to do so in the form in which the story has already dealt with them, a form that, if it was organized logically, in a manner that was too literary, might rather quickly be corrupted and no longer have the least bit of "magnetizing" value. But just as he can always abruptly abandon the theme—if it risks, at a time when the other elements have not reached sufficient maturity, being manifested too exclusively and too openly—then return to it, always in a different *form*, so that the "literary" accomplices might be reduced to a minimum, he finds it again at its true evolutionary point, without alibi and without false light.

The Theme of Childhood

Near the beginning of the book, in the third stanza, Ducasse writes: "I shall set down in a few lines how upright Maldoror was during his early years, when he lived happy. There: done" (29). The "done," an ironic, biting break, indicates that the past actually does not want to have its say. The theme of childhood, in fact, disappears from canto I. Not completely, however. It is manifested, in a disguised manner, in the form of memories or recollections: "By moonlight near the sea, in isolated country places, one sees (when

sunk in bitter reflection) all things assume yellowish shapes, impre-
cise and fantastic. ... In days gone by, borne on the wings of youth,
this made me dream, seemed strange to me ... " (34). "One day my
mother, glassy-eyed, said to me: 'Whenever you are in bed and hear
the dogs' howling in the fields, hide under the covers, don't deride
what they do; they thirst insatiably for the infinite, like you, like
me ... " (36). "Not long ago I saw the sea again and trod the decks
of ships, and my memories are as green as if I'd left the sea only yes-
terday"(37). And of course nothing proves that these recollections
are authentic, but, distorted or not, they nonetheless reveal the fear
of these days gone by as well as the need to recall it. An insidious,
masked need that is not openly welcomed in the text, but makes
itself felt only parenthetically or demands a guarantee from literary
models. In this way it becomes apparent in the family portrait of
stanza XI (44–49), which clearly imitates Goethe. This emulation
is like a trap into which the author lets himself fall, because it is
directed toward convincing him that "literature" alone is in ques-
tion—and nothing else. It is in this scene that Maldoror, conform-
ing to his role, throws himself into this, first to seduce a young
child. But if Maldoror, looking to carry the young Edward away, is
the Lautréamont of tomorrow returning to the Ducasse of earlier
days, is the Ducasse of today tormenting his own memory, we
guess that in reality it is the child and childhood that are tempta-
tion the tempter, excited by the innocence of the seductive images
he puts forth and that encourage in him, in the guise of *Märchen*,
the nostalgic regret for an idealized past.[60] As the canto progresses
it becomes more and more difficult to push it aside, to erase the
memories of the earlier happy days. The "done" is no longer
enough to drive them away. We can easily imagine our childhood
as dead, but such a death always manages to be shrouded in doubt.
Has the young Edward, strangled by the seducer with "a cry of
boundless irony," expired? "If the power the infernal demons have
granted him (or rather that he summons from within himself) is
effective, then before the night slips by this child should be no
more" (49). "If the power ... is effective. ... " Thus the ironic cry
reaches, before any other, the one who hurls it.

And so appears—as if inadvertently, in an enumeration that, behind a rigorous appearance, authorizes a dangerous instinctive impulse—the allusion to the violent incident that puts an end to childhood:

> When a boarder at a *lycée* is ruled for years (which are centuries), from morning till night and night till morning, by an outcast of civilization whose eyes are constantly upon him, he feels tumultuous torrents of an undying hatred mount like heavy fumes to his head, which seems about to burst. From the moment he was hurled into prison, until that time near to hand when he will leave it, a high fever yellows his face, knits his brows, and hollows his eyes. At night he muses, because he does not want to sleep. By day his thoughts vault over the walls of the abode of degradation, toward the moment when he escapes this perpetual cloister or they expel him from it like one stricken by plague... (50–51)[61]

This is neither a divergence nor a pretext. The resentment of Ducasse, who is rejected by his family and locked up in the prison of the college, is expressed in the most direct way: we will know, now, when he throws into his fables the image of prison, which is one of his meanings, one of his sources; we see how prison, once the family is lost, is everywhere, because it not only upsets "the boarder at a *lycée*" to see himself locked up "in the perpetual cloister," it upsets him no less to leave it, being everywhere outside himself. From this we know both sides of his resentment: "undying hate," "his head that seems about to burst," but also the infinite waiting, the stupefaction, and the patience of a slow fever, through the course of which the deliberate intention to see clearly appears for the first time, the implacable refusal of sleep—"At night he muses, because he does not *want* to sleep" (51).

What is remarkable in this confiding is its aspect as an enclave within a text wherein it has no place.[62] Something was said that should not have been said. Thus, in canto II, when the theme of childhood becomes the principal theme, if the same resentment is affirmed, it is beneath a disguise that changes its character. The scene about the omnibus, a burlesque fantasy, is justified solely by this need to talk, which is also a need to conceal: the child who pursues the "Bastille-Madeleine" is the child rejected from the familial bosom ("My parents have abandoned me" [65]), the adolescent seeking in vain to return to the past, ("I've made up my mind to return home" [65]). The obsession is therefore always rather strong. But it is no longer possible to return, and the farcical omnibus, wherein egoism and indifference transform the travelers into turtles and dead fish, is like a dream invented to deflect onto humanity in general the responsibility for his abandonment and simultaneously to delineate the irreducible distance from childhood, because, even as he runs, the child is already no more than a "formless mass."

Ducasse's complicity with childhood, sometimes openly acknowledged, is sometimes seen lurking behind his repulsion for what grows up. If "the ten year old girl" who, in the new stanza, pursues Maldoror with tenacity (a pursuit in every way similar to the pursuit of the omnibus), is really only ten years old, her appearance is thereby friendly, she is slim, her eyes are "engaging and inquisitive," she has "childish charm" (67). But if this naïve face is but a mask, if, by chance, she were twenty years old? "Horrible! Horrible!" answers Maldoror. Hence, we see under which mask appears the idea that childhood is lost, that time passes, is lurking: the child on the omnibus is eight years old, the little girl ten years old, and then abruptly she is eighteen years old, maybe twenty, and Maldoror's sympathy becomes a sadistic hate, wildly eager to annihilate this adult presence. Visibly, the theme "matures," as does he. He begins to reveal more: the kind of anguish, of aberrant vertigo that drives the imagination to associate adolescence with some strangely gendered figure. When Maldoror sees a little girl, he already perceives in her the "horrible" and dangerous form of a completely grown-up girl. The risk of growing up, from that moment on, assumes the dreadful form of a truly other existence.

Now Ducasse is going to cautiously turn this idea of maturity around, so that the new scene of temptation that follows, if it is simply the scene from the first canto returning, is also different. The child has left the family, he is outdoors ("How nice he is, this child seated on a bench in the Tuileries Gardens!" [69]). There is no longer any question of killing him, but rather of expanding him with an impassioned frenzy that, at worst, will last three days. Maldoror's advice is intended less to corrupt him than to make him stronger, to arm him against the injustice of grown-ups, to prepare him to "make your own justice" (70). From the perspective of *experience*, we can consider these theoretical developments as signaling more a backward turn, and it is true that the Ducasse of canto II is not free of the intention to write a book on "the problem of evil"; but it is also true that the desire to see clearly permeates this problem, which is no longer such a theoretical enigma, but becomes, taking root in the unhappy depths, a path leading from the outside inward. Moreover, it goes without saying that when we employ the terms "experience," the "desire to see clearly," and some of our other expressions, we are making use of words that are far too categorical, although hardly fixed. What do we know about Lautréamont? Only this: that he is writing a book and that through this book something in him is being expressed that slowly receives a figure, shifting from one form to another, in such a way that this speech becomes continuously more ample, more profound, and more conscious of its powerful origins. We cannot ignore that a large part of canto II gravitates around the theme of childhood: a child ejected from childhood by his own family, by the fatality of age; childhood that discovers the cruelty of man, the cruelty of God (in the stanza about God's cruel repast); childhood slipping away from itself, en route to adolescence, as if suspended between masculine and feminine natures and, because of this, condemned to solitude (in the stanza about the hermaphrodite); childhood within which the happiness of an initial understanding is revealed and for which knowledge represents the first valuable means toward leaving the self, toward growing up, but sheltered by the world, because this knowledge is itself a separate and cold world (in the stanza about mathematics— "During my childhood, you appeared to me, one moonlit May night ... " [84]); childhood that, in the end, recognizes the oppression of superior powers, God, grown-ups, remorse, and, within the lie of prayer, is taught to form a duplicitous soul, in pushing the reality of evil outside the self, the intimacy of which up to now happiness assured (in the stanza about prayer—"Hear, mankind, the thoughts of my childhood, when I used to wake ... " [90]). This entire "logic" no doubt helps the progression of the stanzas, but it is not the logic that is really important, or it ceases to have any importance when it is reduced in this way to an organizational plan. If, on the contrary, renouncing our consideration of this logic as an abstract idea of unification, we truly want to recognize it as the work of a power that, through variations on a common theme, prepares other even stranger ideas, tests figures, augments the crystallizing violence of language, intensifies words, makes them more charged with meaning and more unstable, and changes them into constellations, the diffused radiation of which is like a light emitted from below the horizon, we will better comprehend that this particular stanza does not contain the development of a certain theme that one might follow and discover again later in the book, because this theme, which ostensibly rears its head (and which we so easily decipher because we isolated and labeled it), is also the movement and the future of the entire work.

Provoking Metamorphosis

The notion of themes is dangerous when it extracts from a text only the sheen of its surface. It is of little interest to note that the episode about lice, blight, curses, and the worry of youth takes its place in this same continuum on childhood or even that it ironically turned into the cannibalistic image of the Creator (because the infinitely small, which, like the infinitely large, devours beings, is, like him, their sovereign leader). Poetically, it is already more important to recognize, between the charming and discreet praise of the hermaphrodite and the praise of mathematics, a curiously similar light, and, in both worlds—slowly rising, in such a way that the young being *doubles* (in whom both preceding images have melded, the image of the child from the omnibus and the image of the little ten-year-old girl), who is described to us at once

as crazy and enriched by all the human sciences,[63] but condemned
to isolation and to the misfortune of powerlessness (sung, it is
true, like a fairy-tale)—is now affirmed, in "the grandiose trinity,"
"the luminous triangle," arithmetic, geometry, the magical powers
of which have overcome, says Lautréamont, everything that was
"vague," "dull" in his mind: we therefore rediscover, in this "initi-
ation,"[64] madness but madness overcome, knowledge having
become a means of combat, a power capable of conquering the
Omnipotent, and finally the solitude of a "virginal" and sepa-
rate—abstract—world, which is however strength and happiness.

We can refuse to see that this progression from stanza to stanza
marks the progress of a power at work. We may judge it preferable
to attribute a movement that holds itself up as superior to every
justification to the arbitrariness of pure creation. But assigning
this role to fantasy is no more poetically legitimate than exagger-
ating the part played by the logic of the themes. From the poetic
point of view, it is perhaps valid to seek no "reasonable" connec-
tion between one such episode and another. But, from this same
point of view, when one sees Maldoror, in canto I (in the stanza
about death), suddenly appear above men as "an appalling comet,"
in the "blood-stained space" (44), an image that conforms to his
superhuman role, then, from stanza to stanza and from canto to
canto, this same image is transformed while persevering—[to the
little girl, Maldoror appears as "a burning comet;"[65] the hermaph-
rodite's hair, which one must not touch, is the asteroid's halo;[66]
swarms of lice, sovereigns of the head, kings of the whole head of
hair, hurl themselves up to the top in the air and become stony
meteorites;[67] "vengeful eyes" of consciousness, which stalk man
everywhere while "extending a livid flame," "ignorant science"
"calls" them "*meteors*" (102); the "imaginary beings," Leman,
Lohengrin, Lombano, Holzer, shine "with a radiance emanating
from themselves" and "die stillborn, like those sparks whose rapid
extinction the eye strains to follow" (107); later, a head of hair will
be charged with an openly erotic meaning and the hair, separated
from the head, will become the helpless witness of scenes of
debauchery, while simultaneously becoming the memory of pow-

erlessness;[68] again later, Maldoror's crime par excellence, the crime whose evocation moves him deeply, to the point that we no longer know if he believes he is guilty of it because he was only a victim of it, is a crime against the head of hair—"I grasped him by the hair with an iron grip and whirled him aloft so quickly that his scalp remained in my hand ... " (157)—an image wherein we again find the two elements, the centrifugal movement and the hair, both of which are already present in the figure of the comet;[69] through to the last image in *Maldoror*, when Mervyn, far from being the victim of a simple, instinctive aggression, becomes the hero of a methodical grand finale and is seen projected into the sky, after a majestic evolution, "a comet trailing after its flaming trail" (218). When we recognize not only the perseverance of such an image, but its transformations, which are not arbitrary, but always oriented in an even more expansive and more dramatic direction, when we see how, around it, all the ideas, all the obsessions and even the turbulent form of the book come to be acknowledged, we must recognize, in the successive stanzas, something other than purposeless inventions of an irresponsible fantasy, but rather the movement of a pursuit that is going somewhere, "toward the unknown."

Considered as a variation on the theme of childhood, the episode about the lice shows nothing more than Ducasse's burlesque power magnificently purging a bad childhood memory and ingeniously celebrating the sovereignty of the head represented by mathematics. But Ducasse is not just an inventor of fantasy, or a clever author piercing an endless stream of subterranean paths from one text to another, and we discern that what is happening is much more serious. This kind of allegory of filth, this apology for "the revolting virginity" (an inversion of the hermaphrodite's luminous virginity), culminates in movements inscribed with a signification that lacks a relationship to manifest things. The immense filth sets out, it lives—and, through it, one of the strangest forces in *Maldoror* takes shape: something inert, dull, immobile, a slowing down of time, sleep in the middle of the day, the slow rumination of a stupefying, decomposing force. The

louse is not happy rapidly sucking blood like the rhinolophus[70]—
the suction becomes a never-ending movement, a patient prolifer-
ation that permeates the light of day, projecting itself, from sub-
terranean depths, into the world above and changing into a sti-
fling and oppressive mass. Beneath this heavy density, language
dulls itself. Through the "hideous" contemplation, a substance
both alive and dead arises, a serpent of "mercury" that exerts the
most dangerous fascination on words: undoubtedly a dreadful
imminence is revealed as a possibility we anticipate. Later, we will
again sense this possibility, but in another light (in the stanza
about the shipwreck [93–99]). There, instead of time falling
beneath time, the raging power that, destroying everything, is able
to rise above and beyond every form and every length of time, will
be acknowledged. In canto I, we witness the ambiguous anger of
the ocean; here the tempest becomes, unequivocally, the madness
shared between man and the ocean: Maldoror's boundless hatred,
"ecstasy," fury great enough to be thought capable of "annihilating
the laws of physics."[71] Further, this elemental frenzy, this violence
that throws him outside human limitations, opens up for him for
the first time, though under the guise of the moral analogy, a
quick and decisive way out, toward quite another existence. "The
long, chaste, and hideous coupling" (99) with the female shark
turns Maldoror into a murky, gooey mass surrounded by fumes of
rotting vegetation.[72] This does not last long and the stanza quick-
ly concludes. But the event sufficiently marks the light in which
hope appears, or the threat of this other existence, the movements
of which associate it with erotic anguish, and how the image of the
ocean, from the "claw" side of the violent sea to "jerky and nerv-
ous movements," then through its silt-laden depths, the murky
water of its reality, reunites both aspects of the experience, is a
constant provocation toward metamorphosis, whose groundwork
is being laid.

During the shipwreck, Maldoror, with his musket, bashed the
head of a sixteen-year-old adolescent, in his aristocratic and bold
face. The following stanza shows us his corpse, but it is now a
body drowned in the Seine, passing time and again under the

arches of bridges, as in another stanza wherein the lamp from a cathedral with the silver burner, the angel against which Maldoror is fighting, follows the course of the current from the Pont d'Austerlitz to the Pont de l'Alma (86–90). Until then, Ducasse had unsuccessfully attempted to begin the story of the fraternal couple; every time he expected to sketch it out, an abrupt break or a digression returned him to the "chaos."[73] A singularly difficult birth. The theme is, in its own way, a young dying boy who must be continuously resuscitated, and it will take the whole effort of three other cantos to lead it, finally, into full-fledged reality. Now, the strange, erotic surge that "the long, chaste, and hideous coupling . . . of brother to sister" represents, makes a new attempt at this theme possible, but through the most discreet images: "the mysterious brother" is at first nothing but a cadaver, an unknown corpse. Maldoror brings him back to life through undoubtedly rather equivocal maneuvers[74]—the fable authorizes them—and when the blond, asphyxiated corpse, who is only seventeen years old, coming back to life, allows himself to be recognized as the dearest of friends, the notion of the crime committed against him—real or erotic—is completely skipped over,[75] in such a way that Maldoror's action assumes the appearance of a magnificently virtuous act ("How fine to save a life! And how the act atones for sins!" [101], words through which irony slips, if one really wants to understand the ambiguous meaning of "this act."). All this happens within the clarity of a "literary" *récit*. Then, both friends riding off *together*, abruptly the stanza ends, and we enter into the most somber language in *Maldoror*. The words soon fall into the semidarkness of insomnia; they get stuck, and their effort to track down obscurity only results in an endless pursuit, in the inconsistency of a dream that transforms itself as soon as you touch it, in the fatality of a death that is always its own resurrection, in the fatigue of sleep at the heart of which the impossibility of sleep is discovered. What is shocking is that the previously described episode, virtuous as it was, now gives birth to reprisals of the most dreadful remorse and, a no less marked return, the same image of the drowned body reappears, this time neither pure nor honest,

but carried away by a lugubrious river wherein immense, tene-
brous spermatozoa flow. Everything happens as if the drowned
body, whom Maldoror has just resurrected, continued its existence
as a corpse and revealed its true nature to us in the implacable
light of remorse and consciousness, a tragic light that essentially
renders death and sleep impossible.[76] Men flee this "livid flame" in
vain. This miserable "human antelope" in vain tries to push his
head "in the earthy intricacies of a hole"; "like a drop of ether the
excavation evaporates" (102). Or, better yet, he throws himself
from the top of a promontory into the ocean, and, "Now for the
miracle: the next day the corpse reappeared on the surface of the
ocean, which bore this fleshy flotsam back to shore. The man freed
himself from the mould of sand hollowed by his body, wrung the
water out of his dripping hair and dumbly, with lowered brow,
resumed life's journey" (102). If this man does not succeed in hard-
ening himself in order to elude the vengeful clarity, it is also to no
avail that Maldoror seeks to abolish consciousness. Terrible strug-
gle. Certainly, he overcame his enemy, he reduced consciousness
to nothing, he "hounded the woman [consciousness] from my
house," he drowned her, he gnawed into her skull, but he must
always annihilate more. Intending to shatter consciousness, he
throws himself, along with it, from the top of a tower: a profound
dream-fall. Then he "gathers" it up, extracts it himself from the
abyss, he resuscitates it in whatever way, because he still wants to
make it a witness to his crimes. An infinite contradiction: the free-
dom of the crime demands the disappearance of such a witness,
but the possibility of the crime demands its survival. Necessarily,
the death of consciousness always has the consciousness, continu-
ously revived, of death on its horizon. This scene too cannot end:
three times, Maldoror places her head under the guillotine; three
times, he triumphs over the guillotine's blade, a victory over the
knife that also *definitively* marks the impossibility of *ending* it.

Such a continuum of images, of extreme dream-like saturation,
indicates the extent to which the degree of discord that we so
calmly called Lautréamont's fight for the light of day, his will to
see clearly, rises. Lucidity,[77] too pure a word, appears here in its

perverse duplicity, as the gaze that gives birth to the crime and the crime itself, which has the intimacy of the eye, which makes the most righteous view guilty, an accomplice to that which it condemns. It also appears, as we foresaw, that Lautréamont's experience seems to drive him to an inexorable contradiction: seeing clearly, diminishing sleep and dreams, slowly drawing the reality of "evil" out into the open, yes, without a doubt, necessarily—but, simultaneously, the uneasiness of a radical transformation is fascinating and attractive to him, when, be it anguish, desire, or methodical will, he must slip "into the maw of space," into "the intermittent annihilation of the human faculties." The human antelope would also really like to become a wreckage of the flesh, an earthy block, and this precisely in order to flee the light of day and shake off a consciousness "that does not err" (102). A flight that is the common lot, carried out in misery, terror, and cowardliness. Maldoror's role is to substitute the provocative decision, an act of defiance and struggle, for this flight. "I defied death and divine vengeance with a supreme howl" (104). The "struggle" is therefore truly an audacious affirmation of sovereignty, and assuredly it leads him to struggle in a certain way against lucidity, to track down and to strike the "hollowed corpse" of consciousness, but so as to make a new light spout from it, the "remaining scraps of intelligence" that the Creator did not want to give man.[78] Finally, Maldoror's mysterious attack against his head, his neck bared three times to the knife of the guillotine that shook him "to his core," is like a tragic experiment to have done with his lucidity, but also to save it, a gloriously surmounted experiment, from which he emerges unharmed, if "without hope," and with one last consent to die on his lips. Thus, there really was a victory, since the head resisted being lost, though the loss was also desired; this is why victory is hopeless. Hence the somber, resigned words that conclude canto II: "It can't be helped if some furtive shadow, roused by the laudable aim of avenging the humanity I have unjustly attacked, surreptitiously opens the door of my room and, brushing against the wall like a gull's wing, plunges a dagger into the ribs of the wrecker, the plunderer of celestial flotsam! Clay may just as well dissolve its atoms in this manner as in another" (106).

Lautréamont and God

Lautréamont's relationship with God is marked by this strange fact: the part of his work wherein eroticism is the most directly present is also the part wherein God plays the most active role. In the famous stanzas wherein God is invoked by turns as the Creator, the Almighty, and the Celestial Bandit, give way to a drinking binge and to the most villainous debauchery, the apparent intention of all this is to associate what is the most high with acts of which man—and especially an adolescent—is reputed to be the most ashamed. The apparent intention nevertheless remains mysterious. The suppressed memory of a degrading story floats over such scenes, and everything sinks into this degradation. At the same time, in the depths of this degradation, it seems that there is an endless exceeding, a superhuman possibility that can only be expressed through the evocation of an irreducible transcendence. God falling into drunkenness, into prostitution, is undoubtedly the adolescent who, giving himself over to these immoral states, seeks to drag supreme morality there, so that, destroyed, this morality can no longer judge him. But Lautréamont also attributes a transcendent meaning to these states, recognizing therein the equivalent of divine vision.

The God in *Maldoror* is the most mistreated in literature. All crimes and all vile acts are attributed to him. He is a kind of sovereign cannibal, priding himself on human excrement, his feet in a filthy pond. To the fall of Lucifer, to the fall of man, Lautréamont adds the divine fall. This great existence is no more than a beggar to whom one offers alms. Sovereignty even fell so low that Maldoror comes to take his side in this last fiery remnant: "O human beings, you are *enfants terribles*; but I beg you spare this Great Being who has not yet done sleeping off the effects of filthy liquor... Oh! You will never know how difficult a thing it becomes, constantly to be holding the reins of the universe!" (120).

Surprising compassion, but it is veiled by an impenetrable irony, because it is also a final way to thwart this great enemy while taking him to be equally worthy of pity, which is however destined to humiliate him even further. In this sense, Lautréamont's God is much more dead than the dead God, and "alone, somber, degraded, and hideous," he has "crossed the boundaries of heaven," a rhinoceros riddled with bullets, an old man reverted to childhood, frightened by his own scandals, piteously subjected to Satan's reproaches, he verges upon the ridiculous and immoral figures associated (we are told) by Kafka with the memory of lost transcendence. In fact, what is the result of this fall? Nothing, and when God, returning to the scenes of his crimes to try to erase any remaining trace, recommences his virtuous lies and shifts to man the penitence for his own misdeeds, it is assuredly a question of one final blow to morality, though he also extracts the certainty that, as low as the story goes, the dialogue between good and evil can only continue unperturbed.

There is an enigma about God in *Maldoror*. It does not however seem that this enigma touches directly upon the feelings that Ducasse could have felt for God. Between Kafka and Ducasse, the distance remains immense: herein there is neither a nostalgia for the lost law nor an anguished fright before the power of this empty death.[79] Lautréamont, whose defiance sometimes places him a little above or below God, though most often on a par with him, in reality needs this superior adversary in order to enact a struggle wherein he will surpass himself. Through Him, his fury assumes a superhuman dimension, and he experiments with another possibility, he gauges the momentum needed to overcome an infinite space. Between this Great Being and Maldoror, there is a continuous exchange of situation, of nature, and of power. Sometimes God visibly assumes his place and becomes the magisterial form, but sometimes one can combat and defy obsessions and obscured depths (thus, onto the scene wherein Maldoror dreadfully sacrifices a young girl, with the help of his bulldog, is superimposed the scene of the red lamp: the same distractions of powerlessness are played out on different registers). Sometimes, behind God and therefore shielded, under the cover of this self-motivated God, Maldoror is fulfilled and becomes what he dreams of being. Thus between them a symmetry and even an indecision, which Lautréamont delineates always more consciously throughout *Maldoror* and concludes in the scene of canto V wherein one of them is recognized in the other and each believes the other to be himself.[80] This is why a critic like H. R. Linder can conclude that Ducasse's hero was sometimes at God's service, like the vengeful angels of the Apocalypse, though God is at Maldoror's service, to the point of offering him the fabulous mirror wherein he can contemplate the true dimensions of his dreadful image (because it superbly emerged from his limits).

The extraordinary erotic condensation that occurs throughout canto III and that illustrates how this experience, now, comes little by little to light, also shows that the possibility of an other existence is connected to the desire or to the anguish of this movement. If, across these stanzas, something secret is said, this is understandable. But if something is also hidden, this is no less visible, and "the broad daylight," which intends to clarify "the foul deed" committed against the poor madwoman's daughter, ironically emphasizes that this light is, moreover, a deceptive one. The details that appear after he has flung himself upon the young girl (as into the ocean), Maldoror's deception when he gets up "dissatisfied," a dissatisfaction that seems to follow from a failure,[81] the appeal that he then makes to the bulldog, who gives life and form to the bestiality of these "base" things, finally the madness that alone held the memory of this story,[82] all these allusions, repeated and developed in the scene about the red lamp (where, for a large part of the stanza, the identity of the divine character is dissimulated for us, He is presented as a "distinguished foreigner," as if, for all this time, He were not someone who, it is divulged in the end, had participated in the scene), do not become any clearer, but they are projected onto an immense screen, where, everything appearing on a superior scale, even the "failings" testify to a kind of superpower. Thus the gigantic hair, which Ducasse takes care to describe meticulously so that we cannot ignore its true nature; if, while "the bodily desires of both partners" grow, he himself senses "his strength diminish," if he "collapses" and finally detaches the hair from the illustrious head, this fall, this self-mutilation, becomes an event of fabulous amplitude, the mythic immensity of which completely masks the modest incident that let it occur.[83] It is then significant that, when the Almighty, seeing that he is hardly Almighty,[84] comes to confess his shame, he appears before his "hair," having become, in a way, his conscience, which judges him, as if, throughout the story, the hero discretely revealed that the only possible absolution was to be sought from enigmatic and capricious erotic power. In the end, madness is no less present in this scene; and this madness, which is the madness of the "nuns" shaken by the terrible spectacle, is described to us with particular nuances, like a lucid obsession, a fear that refuses every repression and, through this madness, retaining the meaning and the memory of this madness, contemplates its cause, even its fascination[85]—fear that singularly responds to the image of lucidity fashioned by Maldoror and to the miseries of a consciousness that, being unable to either forget itself or to forget a dark past, cruelly makes another attempt. Through a detail, Lautréamont has suggested that this entire scene, which we are seeing in the present, was in reality a reading of the past, the remembrance of an event that, before being recounted, even before taking place, we might understand through the code of the obscure language ("in Hebrew characters" [122]) that conceals it. The inscription on the pillar, which divulges the unfortunate fate of the genius adolescent to us in advance—he came to spend some carefree moments in the house and was sadly lacerated by the debauched divinity—clearly alludes to Ducasse,[86] and, nevertheless, this story of *yesteryear*, in which he had been a victim, he *presently* watches through the bars of a grilled window, a witness to himself through all the mythical layers of the *récit* in his mind.[87]

The excessiveness that the erotic signs reach is not only an alibi and a compensation. It is through these relations that Maldoror also experiences excess, and this entire fabulous scene, where the organs start to grow, to act of their own accord, where every ribbon of flesh changes and has an obscure, autonomous existence, where gestures take possession of the limbs that execute them, and movements assume shapes, forcing them to become an amorphous substance ready for extraordinary changes, such a scene is the most conscientious preparation for metamorphosis, the premonition of which guides the book. This is clearly indicated: "these unparalleled swaying hips," through which God himself "loses his identity," "a combination forced by both beings, which an incommensurable abyss separates," represents a climax that opens the way for the "transgressing of limits" and, through crime, fury, madness, and degradation, announces "unaccustomed changes," "the basis for mystery." "Royal soul," writes Lautréamont, "surrendered in one forgetful instant to the crab of debauch, the octopus of weakness of character, the shark of individual abasement, the boa of absent morals, and the monstrous snail of idiocy!" (128). If these are the images, we see, through their common origin, through their nature, which returns each image to a similarly viscous, proliferating existence, capable of indefinite and substantial growth, automatic and indeterminate, how these moral metaphors, while signifying a two-fold physical oppression, from within and from without, strongly attract the being to the heart of metamorphoses, in the milieu the most charged with elementary powers, origin of formless depths and of limitless reality.

Mutation of Language

Faced with such a horizon of change, it is inevitable that *the cantos* encounter the moment when they themselves change and when the attempt, up to now only grazed, toward a radical transformation becomes a conscious attempt and a methodical experience. From the beginning of canto IV, the victorious rapidity of the attack indicates that the time has come: "A man or a stone or a tree is about to begin the fourth canto" (131). And almost immediately Lautréamont opens himself to images that push him toward this change, while clarifying its nature. "When the foot slithers on a frog, one feels a sensation of disgust; but one's hand has barely to stroke the human body before the skin of the fingers cracks like flakes from a block of mica being smashed by hammer blows ... " (131). The foot slithering on the reptilian and batrachian reality, this cold, clammy, and penetrating touch, is the beginning of a feeling of horror, inspired by the human body, and he who experiences it sees himself as changed, through the disgust that he feels, within the object of his disgust, becomes viscous like this thing, becomes this thing. At this moment language also succumbs to a new anxiety, and the labyrinth that it seeks to be, the solemn and endless progression of words, images that, at the very moment when the syntax, continuously slower, seems to be lost in lassitude, follow, on the contrary, an ever more rapid rate, so that we no longer have the time to experience them completely and we leave them unfinished, acknowledging them less for what they signify than for their movement, the continual passing of one into another, a passage even more violent than the contrast of these images, though always linked together by the strong coherence of the discourse and by a secret connivance: such disorder, such order, such an effort to use logic to distract and in order to push speech a little outside of its meaning, implies the imminence of a transformation, after which language will itself have stepped into another existence. Irony, throughout canto III, has already deeply changed its nature. A kind of reservoir, of distant reserves, intervenes in the description of the less habitual events. The crazy mother, recounting her daughter's torture, speaks with a modest and icy good nature. The closing speech, pronounced by the great Satan against God, after the excesses to which he succumbed, alludes to them like completely ordinary grievances: "He said he was greatly amazed ... He said that the Creator ... conducted himself with considerable levity (to say no more)" (127). Thus the derangement of a situation is manifested, wherein the biggest mistake can only give rise to reproaches expressed in a benign tone.

Here irony takes itself for its object. And *Maldoror*, the poetry of *Maldoror*, takes itself as its object. While language seems to want to develop outside of clear consciousness, a consciousness extended further around the work recomposes itself. It is the work that contemplates itself and ironically affirms itself since only irony, from slip to slip, through each experiment it made of a simultaneity of possible meanings, each kept apart from the others, can take possession of this distance and make it visible. And these digressions, these bifurcations, and this perpetual error within which poetry is recovered and announced,[88] do not conceal the fact that they pertain to a secret around which the words turn, all the while without daring to come close to it. Naturally, one is tempted to specify more than would be required. But when one sees Lautréamont, after having grasped the image of the two pillars, which are also two baobabs and two pins (and which would later become the terrible gallows of erotic torture), lose himself in crazy discussions about how to kill bugs and rhinoceroses, when all of a sudden we hear him suggest that this "frivolous" subject is developed in place of "a knotty problem ... of internal pathology," then, having, along the way, neglected to talk about the rhinoceros, acknowledging, shamelessly full of innuendo: "This unpremeditated omission, which will astonish no one who has seriously studied the real and the inexplicable contradictions that inhabit the lobes of the human brain" (135). It is difficult not to be troubled by this allusion, because at the end of *Maldoror*, there will justifiably be an attempt to really kill the "rhinoceros," in whom God has then found refuge and, along with God, all the serious powers of maturity, all the authorities of the world and of the netherworld.[89] If he accordingly forgot to examine here how, after having killed the flies, he could kill the interesting pachyderm, this "unpremeditated omission," which he presents as "inexhaustible food for thought," appears as the strange apparition of forgetting, conscious of what is forgotten and dissimulating its serious meaning behind this very consciousness.

In the middle this prologue, wherein he seems to be happy saying whatever suits his fancy, Lautréamont all of a sudden writes tragically: "The idea that I have *voluntarily*[90] fallen as low as my fellow men, and have less right than anyone else to utter complaints about our lot (which remains shackled to the hardened crust of a planet) and our perverse soul's essence, pierces me like a forge nail" (132). And again: "One has seen fire-damp explosions annihilate entire families; but their sufferings were brief because death was almost instantaneous amid the rubble and poisonous gases: *I* exist forever, like basalt!" (132). And then this: "In the middle as in the beginning of life, the angels resemble themselves: how long ago it is since I resembled myself! Man and I, immured in the limits of our intelligence" (132). A text with a moving subtlety that shows that at this moment, at every level in the book, on the level of theoretical reflection as in the imaginary regions, the movement that is in play is caught once again in its contradictions and its impossible demands. The idea of willful degeneration, an idea not calmly contemplated, but piercing like a forge nail, and as such it seems likely to break off, through horror, the condition of which it however confirms the indestructible permanence. The passion for change becomes the passion for nothingness. The feeling—making this change and this nothingness impossible—of an existence forever hardened, and this eternity of stone that is our own, also pronounces the powerlessness of the freedom of the mind, because this freedom is itself only a prison; likewise, the absence of identity that strikes us confirms our degeneration without rendering us free. Here we feel the particular knot that is tightening around Lautréamont. The fear of "the fellow man,"[91] which traverses the work, does not express only the solitude of the Being separated from others: it indicates the desperate search for a communion, for a fraternal exchange, in other words, for unchanging union. Simultaneously, the contradiction that arises from both these lamentations, significantly placed one after the other—"*I* exist forever, like basalt!," "How long ago it is since I resembled myself!"—shows where, in a certain way, this need to get out of one's self comes from: it is within the self, which is forever lost, an allusion to the nostalgia for the mythic identity, which the plenitude of the ocean already expressed, the memory of childhood, the horror of the duplicity symbolized by prayer, a duplicity that is hypocritically insinuated everywhere and, having become the universal law, in the name of God, men, good, evil, through demands for clarity, through tricks with mirrors, introduces even in our-

selves separation and dissemblance. It does not however seem that
the romantic idea of paradise lost had a positive meaning for
Lautréamont, nor that it represents an exemplary ideal salvaged
from the universal wreckage. If Maldoror conserves, within him-
self, as the root of his feelings and the justification of his atrocities,
the memory of a far-off existence not separated from him, his
effort does not intend to go back but to find, within the present
moment, wherein all is separate and divided, by ripping every-
thing apart, through excesses, through trials and tribulations, like
a negative fullness and an escape hatch into the void. Assuredly,
the fraternal reconciliation with others is a nagging impulse in
him—"Two friends stubbornly trying to destroy one another,
what a drama!"—but as this desire seems to have its source in an
event blurred by its own telling, an event that poisons precisely
this source and causes this desire to be, not the calm appeal of sim-
ilarities, but the decomposing and furious delirium of another
existence, as a result, the reconciliation is nothing more than an
aspect of the discord, and its impossible desire only renders the
search for it more absurd.

When we say that the same movement, throughout the work he
is writing, leads Lautréamont to shed fresh light on his dark rever-
ies and to uncover, in the very horror where, when he slips, he sees
himself torn from his limits, a new possibility that he demands,
that he proclaims, and that he pursues, in the end, as a voluntary
experience, we say nothing that he does not say himself, but this
would be to misunderstand the nature of such a movement, which
would like to precisely distinguish the moment when the horrific
slipping is triumphantly recovered, like a concerted project, with-
in the experience of the metamorphosis. Just as lucidity is not cold
theoretical reflection, and as it permeates so profoundly the dark-
ness wherein it seems to lose itself while it is discovering this very
darkness, just as what is voluntary in this impetus, which he takes
as falling outside of himself, remains inseparable from the anguish
that drove him there, from the malaise that led to it, in other
words, from the powers most likely to stupefy every decision and
to infect a liberated desire with fatality. But only this vertigo

remains: at a certain moment, Lautréamont makes it his own, and this almighty adhesion assures, in the beyond of degradation and in those zones wherein all personal stability is shattered, the maintenance of his sovereignty and the coherence of his incredibly extended mind.

The Two Dispositions of Metamorphosis

The first words of stanza XXXIX are "I am filthy" (142). Since the episode about the lice, when colossal filthiness was set in motion, it certainly made strange advances. Now Maldoror, immobilized in the earth by the tenacity of his own inertia, a tree riddled with parasites (like the body of the unfortunate hanged man in the preceding stanza, but his hanging having become his strength), has transformed himself into a collective system of animal lives, all of which are issued "from the kingdom of viscosity": toad, chameleon, viper, crab, jellyfish. The first attempt is outdated, as we have seen; Maldoror, deep in shadow, turns his head slowly left and right, "for hours on end." Here we have four centuries of immobility, voluntary immobility, which has suspended time and, at the heart of a passivity similar in every way to death, has retained an unwavering tension, so that the decomposition of the Being, through numbness and sleep, is insidiously taken into account as a deliberate attempt. Lautréamont did not stop having this premonition: if the paroxysm of frenzied violence, while producing a rupture, can tear him from himself, the power of an infinite passivity, in suppressing time, is no less capable of encountering the undetermined moment between life and death when the same disappears and the other approaches—a double possibility the progressive experience of which is the profound experience of *Maldoror*. Here, it is nevertheless "hatred," "stranger than you think," rebellion and the will to fight that transformed him into this cadaverous Job, again an uncertain cadaver.[92] But that the will, the apparently free decision, is partly a prisoner, or "the vow to live diseased," "until I had overcome the Creator," is also diseased, this is what Lautréamont will discover later and what he declares from this moment on with the strange episode of the double-edged sword, vertically impaled through his loins by a man who silently came up from behind him.[93] Now this blade is stuck so deeply into his body that no one is able to extract it, not the philosopher or the doctors. It truly seems that it might be this blade that restricts him to immobility and that this splitting point lodged in his vertebrae, this gigantic thorn that cannot be withdrawn from his flesh, is like an allusion to the spear of hate, a strange presence, embedded in his past, which he is also seeking to extract, but against which he must voluntarily lean in a certain way in order to remain standing.[94]

When faced with this recollection, the memory buckles. "I do not even remember it clearly," says Lautréamont, and this memory, he reiterates, "is possibly just a dream."[95] But, since the following stanza will dangerously put these intentional refusals to remember to the test,[96] just as it will push further, to the point of hallucination, the distortion of lucidity, all while clearly warning Maldoror that his struggle is a struggle against the self and that he is only projecting his own defects and his own impulses onto his imaginary adversaries, after "this outrageous and silent interrogation," the dream, a kind of alibi that he momentarily allows himself, recognizes in its own right that it is the image, the story of his desire, and then Lautréamont triumphantly accepts the responsibility for this desire in a glorious frenzy that opens up the doors of metamorphosis for him. "I was asleep on top of the cliff" (148). This is the first sleep in *Maldoror* that is enveloped in an immense insomnia. Strange sleep, we said. Sleep mixed with the refusal to sleep, to be fed, to live. It is compared to the catalepsies of magnetism and is, in short, just another expression of the methodical apathy of the "four centuries," during which Maldoror became a tree.[97] At the center of sleep, metamorphosis fully takes form: "It had come at last, the day I became a hog! I tried out my teeth on tree-bark; my snout I contemplated with delight" (149). It is necessary to note, however, that the meaning of such a transformation, whether it is fortunate or unfortunate, still remains undecided: a curse or a sovereign reward? Degradation "inflicted upon me by divine justice" or desire's supreme conquest, "plaguy joys"? Lautréamont affirms both of these, then suddenly he chooses, and, as at his very own highest point, drunk with a degeneration that withdraws every "bit of divinity" from him, elevating his soul "with the excessive height of that ineffable sensual bliss," he pronounces the word that transforms fatalism into freedom: "To my eyes the metamorphosis never appeared as anything but the exalted and magnanimous echo of a perfect happiness I had long awaited" (149). Through this choice of degraded sovereignty, reduced to nothingness, a greeted sovereignty is created, of baseness and of nothingness, from which Maldoror receives unequaled strength. Freed from every law, finally rejecting the hurdle of consciousness,[98] he is the embodiment of power, the intoxication of unrestrained combat: "I was the strongest and gained all the victories" (149). And yet, so great is his lucidity that in the extreme circumstance of this anxiety, when he attains the height of triumph, of movement and joy, this is when he also becomes aware that this movement is immobility, this joy solitude, and this triumph sterile. Thus he falls from metamorphosis through the dream into the simple dream of metamorphosis.[99]

But if the dream has a deeper meaning, it is seen through this feature: transformed into a hog, Maldoror still appears to be caught in a rather course moral allegory. Though, in fact, a strange hog, he described it as an "irreducible mixture of dead matter and living flesh" over which the tide twice passes, while the metamorphosis itself is described as a "frightful flattening against the granite's belly"[100]—an image that refers us back to that of the octopus of the silkenglance in canto I, behind which is Dazet:

> O octopus of the silkenglance! You whose soul is inseparable from mine; you the most handsome inhabitant of the terrestrial globe, who govern a seraglio of four hundred suction cups; you in whom are nobly enthroned as in their natural habitat, by common consent and an indestructible bond, the sweet virtue of communication and the divine graces—why are you not with me, your quicksilver belly against my breast of aluminum, both of us seated on some rock by the shore ... (37)

(Maldoror is there, likewise, "asleep on the top of the cliff.") We can justly say: it is during this very "dream" that Lautréamont's hand recalls the name of Dazet from canto I in order to replace it with the image of the octopus with four hundred suction-cups who has now become, along similar lines, the hog that Maldoror had been changed into, and is also transformed, metamorphosed into this muddy heap, over which the deep forces of the ocean pass.[101]

"To resume, as my right, my ruined metamorphosis" (150), this project is now so apparent that it cannot longer be put off and, from one stanza to the next, it is confirmed, moving from the doubt of the dream to reality. Such is the object, fully aware, of the new stanza, "which contains a monster," one of the obvious centers of the work. It is at this moment, in fact, when Maldoror, still standing on the top of a cliff, sees coming toward him, mixed intimately with the ocean, a human being just like a dolphin, whose metamorphosis is logically shown to us as the correct way for man to expand his horizons: like the free future of humanity. Lautréamont enumerates all the reasons for such an aspiration: moral reasons, freedom from crime, objective reasons, evolution, the appropriation of the place, the instability of the human organism—too complex to be definitively determined—reasons drawn from a poetic dream, a premonition of the possibilities that it places in human existence, at least on the level of the imagination, its agreement with elementary powers, water, air, earth.[102] But the true origin of this project is not here: it is—Lautréamont reveals it in a very explicit manner—in the aberrant states that he himself tested and, through this process, glimpsed the possibility of suspending or of diverting the laws of nature. In this affirmation, once again, both irreconcilable and inseparable positions are implicated, both completely necessary in order to propel Being outside itself: these fits of anger and diseases (patients) of pride, "the forceful pressure of the will" and "the absence of its effective collaboration." And in order to make itself more distinct, the allusion develops, while revealing, in the language of *Maldoror*, the same contrast, in a double aberration of duration, having become at once excessively speedy and infinitely slow.[103]

The amphibian, with its viscous body, its large duck-like feet, surrounded by aquatic strata and schools of fish, once again links the depths of the sea with metamorphosis.[104] Meanwhile, insofar as these images are too specifically and too directly used in shaping a literary fiction, their importance diminishes, so that the metamorphosis is now less where it appears than already dispersed in the world, in the fact that those who see it see the invisible and those who do not see it become others. Furthermore, behind this type of human hope and from the perspective of the future, the premonition of a troubled past slips in, a past that is the origin of it all, as if it were always becoming more certain that to the extent that this past will not have been brought to light, it will render this experience null and void, and as though it were necessary for reason to be made the mistress of its aberrations—which allowed this perspective to appear—not in order to erase them but to overcome them, in other words, to go beyond them. The amphibian is now what is monstrous in the past: "plunged in the past, he resembled a reef" (154). And when he recounted how he sought his freedom within the sea, the sea again seems to want to swallow him up in "former reminiscences of a life lived fatally" (155). The very story the monster tells brings together different themes and images. The progression has remained uncertain up to now. Certainly, when we read how the ill-fated man was lost as a result of his twin brother's jealousy, how his parents, who loved him deeply, were persuaded by the slander of this bad brother, how, then, imprisoned for fifteen years in a dungeon, tortured, he succeeded in escaping by throwing himself into the sea, such a story, drawn from the pure tradition of the popular novel, may seem sufficiently justified by its origin, but it is not as fiction that it is important to us. The theme of the fraternal pair, also taken directly from the tradition of fiction, nevertheless allows us to foretell, by its obsessive nature and the interest that weighs this obsession down, that Ducasse's sensibility is interested in it. In the very conventional story of the amphibian, several previously used elements charged with a burning meaning are discovered: the image of the prison refers us to the college dungeon (wherein, for Ducasse, the very meaning of freedom perished), a prison to which he had been condemned by his parents, and in the attenuating circumstances that the present fable attributes to the father and mother, there exists the memory of a childlike tenderness, a tenderness that, every time he draws a family picture, even with the most parodic intentions, obligates him to continuously modify the cruelty of his descriptions with a certain indulgence. When the amphibian wants to be set free, this freedom will not only consist in getting him out of the dungeon, but, the text says, out of the triple pillory: that of the progressive weakening of the body, that of solitude, and, an unsettling detail, that of his affection for his own people, which suggests that, for Ducasse, being free is firstly freeing oneself of memories and nostalgia for one's childhood.

The Work and the Whirlwind

The image of the secret "crime"[105] that one day penetrated the heart of brotherhood, corrupted it and now makes it a place of hate and regret, is too constant, too permeated with passion not to possess the most important meaning. Which meaning is the most important one? We do not know. Deciphering it would have no other objective than that of bringing it into the realm of common experience, since this obscure incident—perhaps dreamed—is, for Ducasse, unique and concealed from all direct expression. It is this image that *Maldoror* presently tries to contain and that possesses it with unequaled force. Throughout the stanza about Falmer, which closes canto IV, it enters into a new phase: the crime against a brotherly adolescent—broached for the first time in the episode with Lohengrin as an attempt, though dismissed, and briefly mentioned a few pages previously, in the stanza about the mirror—without any possible doubt is fulfilled in a whirlwind of memories that invoke it, simultaneously divulging the passionate meaning of this crime, because henceforth it becomes a crime against hair. One day, Maldoror, grabbing a beautiful blond adolescent fourteen-year-old boy by the hair, "whirled him aloft so quickly that his scalp remained in my hand" (157). The motif of hair—and especially of scalped hair, cut—is one of these "tics, tics, and tics," an obsessive motif that Lautréamont denounces, in his *Préface à un livre futur* (*Preface to a Future Book*), as the fatality of poetry. The gigantic hair, detached from the illustrious head, and the fall of which is at once the punishment of divine excess and the expression of the powerlessness connected to this excessiveness, a bit later becomes the hair of the man hung from the gallows and, more precisely, hung by his hair. "He was howling, 'Who'll untie my arms, my hair? With each move I dislocate my bones, but my hair is severed more sorely from my scalp" (138). This unfortunate man, victimized by two drunk women, "two female orangutans," his wife and mother, sees himself as condemned to be tortured, tarred, and whipped so as to escape incestuous desires. Here *Maldoror*'s irony offers the most intentional of winks at psychoanalysis. The torture not only reveals the horrified recoil before normal sexual relations, but the irony shows that these relations, instead of proceeding on an ordinary level, return to the past and that marriage, conjugally null and void, seeking a union between mother and son, is diverted and monopolized by the dream of an incestuous union, a union that is itself lacking, in such a way that the punishment is also that of impotence. To free the victim, Maldoror cuts his hair.[106] But, in the stanza about the mirror, after having vainly considered his own head as though it belonged to someone else, he discovers himself scalped, and "this meaningful lack of hair," associated with the image of prison,[107] which appears once again, leads to a compensatory reverie of universal destruction. It goes without saying that such transformations must not remain linked to meanings that the theme momentarily appears to welcome. As startling as the "tics" are, more stunning still is the fact that these obsessive figures obey a law of assured development, expanding up to the moment when, having attained maturation, they disappear, absorbed into a more expansive figure. In the stanza about Falmer, the essential event is the merging of the hair motif with the movement of the whirlwind, the centrifugal spinning that will soon be recognized as the very law of composition in *Maldoror*. Everything happens as if the image of hair was here attaining its culminating moment and, shifting with all of its emotional saturation into the simpler, more pure and more comprehensive image of the whirlwind, as if it was now going to be obscurely perpetuated as one of the emotional nuclei of this new image.

Through his work, Lautréamont passes from the implicit to the explicit, from the obscurity of a secret to the clear consciousness of obscurity, then to the clarity of a revelation wherein nevertheless obscurity resides.[108] The sumptuous figure that develops and analyzes the whirlwind flight of the starlings shows this presently. In the stanza about Falmer, the movement of the cyclone is expressed simultaneously within the content of the narration and through its form. The sentences turn according to an order of skillful gyration: the gyrating power inhabits the language, but without being revealed again, other than through its effects. The figure of the multitude of starlings, which opens canto V, overtly considers this power as the power unique to *Maldoror*, explaining, through this power, its strange movement, revealing how its apparent disorder becomes a profoundly methodical progression toward a true order. But this image, which brings to light one of the most obscure particularities of the work, is itself far from becoming transparent. As well as remaining protected by irony, which triumphs immediately thereafter, it only permits the premonition that this movement, which always brings the motifs closer to the center—all while also pushing the center toward the outside (in such a way that language, inspired by a gigantic funnel-shaped movement, progressively closer to the depths, must in the end turn back on itself and project toward the surface the point that designates the extremity of the gyration and of the gulf)—that this two-fold movement is not pure artistic virtuosity, but signifies the effort, one toward the other, of an anomaly and a new rule, the transformation, nearly simultaneous, of aberration into reason and of lucidity into sleep. At the moment when *Maldoror* gives way to progressively stupefying images, when the *Beautiful as's* ensnare language in a climactic outburst of irony relinquishing every equilibrium, Lautréamont, with a true ferocity, confirms the accord of poetry and intelligence, of enthusiasm and inner coldness, or reason and putrefaction, and undoubtedly, with final sarcasm, he shifts the fear of evil or illness onto the reader, as well as the "obstinacy" that runs throughout his work, but it is so that, as the first words of the first canto said, in the end, the reader changes into what he reads.[109]

As we get closer and closer to the moment when the illusion of the gyrating bulge will place what is lowliest on high, and vice versa, we also reach the moment when the narration seems the furthest away from common vision, and yet closest to being completely self-conscious. The animal density in the narration becomes infinitely strong; the air breathed, the most lacking in human molecules. The motifs, the images, raised by the work to their richest concrete point, are brought toward each other, are united in a tightness that renders their unity indissoluble, and their decomposition inevitable. The stanza about the man with the pelican head marks the extreme point of the metamorphosis, and what the stanza has trouble withstanding is completely affirmed. The beetle rolling an excremental ball on the ground with its mandibles and antennas, the object standing on a mound that becomes, with fabulous slowness, a pelican head extended by a human body, the obstinacy of the beetle to push the plastic ball toward the mound, despite all this effort, riddled with sarcasm, has the clarity, at a certain moment, of a "story": the story itself plunges too deeply into a world of images, it is too mysteriously enmeshed in the story of the narration for the illumination it arouses to have the effect of obscuring the light on its own. If the beetle and the man with the head of a palmiped[110] are finally two brothers, if the ball of rot is the body of a woman who has cheated on both of them and who is presently enduring their revenge, this burlesque fiction is in fact becoming more serious. We recognize in this scene the reversal of the hanged-man episode: both shrews, united in one common delirium of vengefulness, resolute in transforming the powerless unfortunate man into a tarry mass, have mysteriously taken the place of these two brothers, implicated also, in a communal erotic deception, as if Maldoror had real-

ly become the brother of the unfortunate man whom he saved, as
if, in addition and more secretly, the tactics of the woman against
the man, his horrible desires, had justified, had invoked the con-
fused fraternity of the virile couple. The woman metamorphosed
both men, and she herself, imprisoned within this excremental
concretion, must now withstand the revenge of those whom she
deceived. A revealing story, but an even more revealing image,
because this sphere, within which we find the atoms of the woman
reduced to putty, "the effects," says the beetle, "of my fiery pas-
sion," is the new concrete form of the whirlwind, the impasto of
this image, impregnated with the most equivocal erotic sensibili-
ty.[111] And if we now lift our head, we see, projected into the sky
by a splitting that is, we now know, one of the laws of the book,
the same image, the same scene, but slightly transformed. While
the beetle and the palmiped hesitate before the spherical amalgam,
between pity and vindictiveness, both characters find themselves,
in the air, in the form of the lamb-eating vulture and the Virginian
eagle-owl, led to fight one another in forceful gyrating flying—
and suddenly, through an unusual intervention, the author, wit-
ness to all these miserable acts, abruptly enters the scene and
decides to stop the fighting. Such strangeness may appear too gra-
tuitous to be explained, which is to say disconnected from their
strangeness, and in effect, strange, these acts must not cease being
so. What is important is not to offer predetermined meanings that
would be easy to affix to these details, but from this movement—
which leads Lautréamont to simultaneously experiment with dif-
ferent forms of the same image, then to push the hazardous incli-
nation further toward splitting—it is more important to acknowl-
edge the sudden effort made to interrupt the experience, as
though through fear, of a premature denouement. Similarly, if the
pelican asks his brother to not push the madness of his molding
course so violently, which more and more transforms a human—
and possibly living[112]—being into an amorphous polyhedron, this
mitigation does not have a moral meaning; but behind this appeal,
when fury, we are told, risks augmentation in irreparable propor-
tions, the warning is audible, a warning that the limit is going to

be attained, a warning that, throughout the work, is destined for the one writing it.

"I Am Not an Other"

At this moment of the most profound transformation, Lautréamont is in fact at the most conscious point in his thought, and this simultaneity of extreme conditions arouses in him such an overwhelming tension that his lucidity becomes sorrowful wailing. How pure reason can become pure suffering, here we understand. "The spirit withers with condensed and continually strained reflection; it croaks like the frogs in a marsh ... " (167). "It is now more than thirty years since I slept" (167). Atrocious insomnia, a wan though unimposed crown that unmitigatedly squeezes the head: praises sung, demanded through the perseverance of the free will. Sleep, "the reduction to a mindless state," the ignoble fate of the Being that is forsaken in oblivion and strays toward darkness, this is what Lautréamont designates to be the great adversary of his struggle, the vicious powers that a "secret and noble justice" "orders me to track down without truce" (168). Never has the struggle for daylight been loaded with more meaning. Struggle, a protestation, in the name of "autonomy," against all external forces, an affirmation of a closed and pure existence, taken as much from the pressure of the world, from the moral investigation, from the tyranny of all kinds of authority as from "the grim curiosity of the Celestial Bandit," from this Great External Object the monumental name of which denounces everything that is a limit, an objection, and foreign resistance. Through the most powerful sentences, Maldoror's pure choice is affirmed for us: "I want to live alone in my intimate reasoning ... My subjectivity and the Creator—it is too much for one brain" (169). An affirmation of a decisive clarity. And, at the same time, we grasp how this pure desire to be one's self, the agonized refusal of every other presence, through this very anguish, becomes the fascinated movement that opens the Being up to the Other and radically changes it into something else. The Rimbaudian phrase,

"If I exist, I am not another" (169), leads immediately to this uneasiness: "Autonomy ... or let me be turned into a hippopotamus" (169). And, naturally, the abstract meaning of this "or let me" is rather clear, it means: insofar as I am a human being, on behalf of free subjectivity I refuse and contest someone else's infinite existence the right to intervene in mine. But this refusal does not only address "the hideous spy on my causality," the Creator, and "this infamous torment" of the curiosity is no less odious when it is provoked by the desire or the investigation of men: it is then even more than that "her modesty's veil undergoes cruel rents" (168), so that we are now returned to the obscure moment when the horror of becoming Other, a horror so much greater than the passion for a pure me, is stronger, and leads, with the leap into the alternative, to the triumphant experience of metamorphosis.

But more must be said: it is obvious that while seeking, with such energy, to push aside the unbearable intrusion of outside forces, Lautréamont shows just how serious and immediately threatening this danger is. That something in him, which apparently is not him, is claiming to control him, or that he then feels like he is "in a stranger's hands," is not unlikely; and the alarming nature of such an enemy, being so close to him and even at the heart of his inner life, suffices to grant a tragically personal meaning to his struggle against all those who are this enemy's representatives, his assistants—though, at the same time, it is thanks to them that he struggles and can hope to be triumphant. The "implacable scalpel" that "probes its dense undergrowth" is here too close to the sharp-edged blade, implanted straight up the length of his vertebrae, which no one was able to pull out; and if he speaks of "the anonymous stigmata" that he is looking to have the ground swallow up, it is in fact that the strangeness he continues to grapple with is nameless, and its infamy that of a mark left by "evil."[113] The truth is that the very will to see clearly, where hunted freedom takes refuge and is concentrated, "atom that is revenged in its extreme weakness," carries within it a principle of death. We know it, but here the experience is pushed to its limit.

Lucidity, drunk with itself, is able to become the haggard equivalent of sleep; lucidity is captivated, is fascinated and, having become its own "deathly" appearance, a piece of tomb behind which, "mesmerized meaning," it re-emerges in order to fully admit it is a prisoner, it always is more bewitching through the contemplation of its powerlessness. Three times, Lautréamont alludes to this, the most dramatic of all moments, when the desire for light characterizes a supreme victory as obscure, the work of reason as delirium, and, when sovereign freedom, having become a foreign fatality, is the very enemy against which it is struggling. He says, "Consequently it is certain that through this strange struggle my heart (starveling that devours itself) has immured its schemes" (168). "Who does not know that when the struggle between the proud self and the terrible progress of catalepsy continues, the hallucinated spirit loses its judgment? Gnawed by despair, it *delights* in its disorder till it has defeated nature ... " (169).[114] We see it, the indulgence in evil, which corrupts the struggle against evil, is also the hope and the way to conquer evil. Already, a little earlier, moving in circles considering the eternal movement of his will, condemned to worry about a perpetual freedom, Lautréamont sarcastically recognized, in nightmares and fantasies about metamorphosis, not the mad work of an anxious will, but instead a way to stabilize this anxiety and to take control of this madness: "know that nightmare, who hides in the phosphorescent corners of the dark, fever that palpates my face with its stump, and every tainted animal rearing its bloody claws—well, it is my will that, to provide steady sustenance for its perpetual activity, makes them revolve" (168). And this is why, at this point, the struggle oscillates between victory and defeat, the stupor of inertia and the lucid will that this stupor perpetuates, between the nightmare, which is nothingness and death, and death, which wants to make this nothingness real. "Impenetrable as giants, *I* have lived ceaselessly with eyes yawning open" (168). But: "Cast a little ash upon my inflamed orbit. Do not stare into my unblinking eye. Do you understand what suffering I endure (though pride is satisfied)? ... I fear my resolution may succumb to the ravages of old age. Let that fatal day come when I shall fall asleep!" (169–70). Livid lucidity, which is "a torrent of molten metal," existence is nothing more than vertical obstinacy: "When dawn breaks it finds me in the same position, my body propped vertically, erect against the plaster of the cold wall," and, meanwhile, not for a moment has been lost "the free faculty of movement" (168). Similarly we find here, though seen in a different "light," Maldoror's strange posture, when, squatting, then standing, he turned his head for entire hours;[115] and likewise the sleep of death, which the clairvoyance, stupefied by itself, becomes, restores several of the images on which the work of *Maldoror* was continuously exerted: that of the sharp-edged blade that immobilized Maldoror ("four enormous stakes nail all his limbs on to the mattress"); that of the tree that he became ("Curious enough, my inert arm has knowingly assumed the stiffness of the stump"); that of the guillotine under whose blade he laid his head,[116] and even the "binary" of the two pillars becoming two baobabs, in the end becoming four, which are here as much the four stakes as "the binary posts of the guillotine" toward which the dream irresistibly leads him. The dream that he will, in the morning, if he perceives that he has slept, make real by truly cutting his throat, thus canceling out the dream by fulfilling it.

The Heart of the Universe

When Lautréamont speaks of "the mysteries in whose midst our life chokes like a fish at the bottom of a boat," when he writes, "It is not enough for the army of physical and spiritual sufferings that surround us to have been born: the secret of our tattered destiny has not been divulged to us,"[117] it is completely true that this secret and this darkness that we must pierce, these "scraps of intelligence" shamelessly hidden in the intestines of the crafty bandit, which it is necessary to bring to light, concern human fate in its entirety, not just Ducasse's particular story. But the secret, if it is everyone's secret, is firstly our own—mine—in the part, lived in obscurity, that is given over to it through every unusual event buried in the past and in this private life of madness that reason, if it wants to be completely penetrated, must necessarily discover within itself. Lautréamont's quest moves through Ducasse's heart, but this heart is also the heart of the universe, and this is why his struggle, if the enemy is obsession, and if the obsession is God, is sometimes reduced to that of his existence grappling with his personal torments, sometimes making these torments the issue and the expression of the universal struggle. On the one hand, the image of God is always closer to being confused with the image of Lautréamont, but on the other hand, Lautréamont always becomes more the measure of the world. In his eternal dialogue with the eccentric python, he senses more and more that this dialogue is only a monologue; that he himself is God; that he gave himself his own ugliness, "fallacious mirage of fright;" and when he condemns "the monarch of the universe" to live rootless, "to remain alone and without family," when he snubs him, saying, "It is too late to weep now,"[118] this unhappy fate and this exile are obviously nothing more than the fate and exile of Ducasse, who, in his desire for revenge, gives them precisely the form that they might assume in another young Being, reprimanded by his father, who would like to snub him, in his own right, treating him like a child. But, if this has brought him closer to God, to the point of no longer being able to distinguish himself from him, he has simultaneously risen to the dimensions of the universe and transformed into cosmic powers the particular tastes that he claims to be his own. The stanza about the "incomprehensible pederasts,"—which, in order to gauge its provocative intensity, we must remember was written, at the latest, in 1869—is not only the culmination of the "filth," or the simple divulging of a fear that let itself be felt, divulgence canceled out by its very outrageousness, but it especially powerfully affirms the transcendent destructive, with cosmic force, particular to eroticism, in which vertigo, anguish, and the fervor of desire have already indicated, through the experience of metamorphosis, the prodigious excess capable of breaking through limits.

> Oh! If instead of being a hell this universe had been but an immense celestial anus—behold the gesture I make, hard by my lower abdo-

men: yes, I would have pushed in my prick through its blood-stained sphincter, smashing the very walls of its pelvis with my impetuous movements! Misfortune would not then have blown into my blinded eyes entire dunes of shifting sand; I would have discovered the sub-terranean place where truth lies sleeping, and the rivers of my viscous sperm would thus have found an ocean in which to rush headlong! (173–74)

A conclusive dream of extreme power wherein we see humanity, attracted by Maldoror's infinite vitality, set out, in his pursuit, from all earthly constraints and devoting itself to a struggle the outcome of which can only be universal destruction: in such a way that, through this struggle, of which besides Maldoror is the almighty cause—though passive, and while absent—eroticism in the end does not appear connected to life, but, ironically, to the bewitchment of sterility and to a hope for the end of the world.[119]

If the will to make use of scandal as a power capable of shaking the world, of provoking universal instability, wherein, led into the anxiousness of an enormous desire, everything would perish, if this will explodes, this provocative affirmation exerts itself no less within Lautréamont himself, against his passions, manifest and concealed, overwhelmed by the excess within which they arise. "I hide covertly in the most inaccessible places" (176), he says strangely, at the very moment when he becomes the object of uni-versal passion and when this passion, not being able to locate him, or to be self-satisfied, is going to become enraged and to provoke the derision of a total destruction. Equally, for the endless strug-gle within him, this is a way to recognize that his chaotic force has its principle in a secret, a hidden and inaccessible memory, and is even more effective since it cannot be located (like those storms and pitfalls that, he says, "are conspicuous only by their under-standable absence").

The Night of Ten Years

"One last word," he says at the end of the stanza. In fact, it is the imminence of this *last word* that, never ceasing to evade in the confession that would like to expose it, inasmuch as we sense, but always in vain, that everything is going to be said and that at the heart of the most radical frankness the lack of an ultimate reserve is still maintained, such an imminence turns the reading of *Maldoror* into a waiting for an impossible end, wherein the demand for a denouement, at whatever price, weighs heavily. The imminence of the denouement is now announced by the "Silence!" with which Lautréamont's imperious voice begins the second to last stanza (176). The veil of death is spread over the *last word*, the secret of this unknown death and of the funeral procession, which however advances solemnly before us, appears connected to the definitive disclosure of which this death is possibly the price. Death, which Ducasse loved to protect affectionately within secrecy, clarifies all the enigmas. Nameless death, "cut off on the borders of boyhood," for "ten years," of which an image of great magnificence, prepared by all kinds of innuendoes, identifies with the beauty of the great flight of the royal kite (thus the figure of the whirlwind is once again apparent), and of this dead one on whom floats the memory of dangerous exotic excesses,[120] Maldoror, transposed for the moment into his role as Horseman of the Apocalypse, follows from afar the burial, as if he were attending, disguised, his own premature interment. "He whom, says the priest of religions, sickness forced to taste only of life's first stages, and whom the grave has just taken unto its bosom, is alive beyond doubt," and this one here (Maldoror), "although he has lived much, is the only one really dead" (180).

It would be too easy to want to see, though Lautréamont tempts us to, this mysterious dead youth as the very childhood of our hero, a childhood that had been life itself for him and whose "abrupt interment" turned his life into a true death. Assuredly, this young corpse haunts *Maldoror*, and when the small shapeless shadow that ran behind the omnibus, at the time when "the juvenile reversal of things" is about to be erased, receives the reward of a grave, this only ties the beginning to the end.[121] But, specifically, the end is only, on the surface, in this grave, which closes up; we are also going to learn that the same duration of ten years is applied to the long night during which Maldoror was a prisoner of a nightmare, and this corpse of the ten-year-old, which he is going, in fact, to bury, will therefore then be the fundamental, spellbinding past from which, thanks to a persistent struggle, he ended by finding a way toward the outside. Tragic sleep wherein the illusion of light never ceases to mislead and that has so many times been compared to the anomaly of death, incapable of ending itself. And now, strange fact, this liquidation of a nightmare past appears, in advance, in this prophetic scene, as a liquidation of the true life and a definitive acceptance of death, such that Lautréamont, at the moment when his work will bring him the victory of clarity and of the revelation about the anguish of the secret, seems to sense the price he must pay for this victory and what death the total triumph of the light, the end of dreams, and the tranquil life of the world signifies.

The Imperceptible Rustling

The word "Silence!" spreads so definitively over the entire text (as death seems to want to pierce it)[122] that, one stanza finished, another that begins like the previous one is still engaged in the same silence, and the only noise that we might hear is an "imperceptible rustling," which is itself silence. This is not the first time the rustling appears. It is one of these faint echoes, within *Maldoror*, that has reverberations every now and then: the hum of metallic wings in the temple of Denderah, a rustling of the three consoles of my pain, a delicate cricket song (131–33), and especially the nearly imperceptible vibrations of the sheet of paper, hung on a wall by a nail, in the room on the fifth floor where the reflective young man has aspirations of glory, when the smoke from the candle agitates the paper, at the calm hour of midnight, an "unaccountable rustling," similar to the noise of the "mosquito's wings," in which Lautréamont, in the end, identifies the "syllables" of the name Maldoror (158). It is this so very slight noise, and as if inside the night, that, slowly constructing a body, now gives birth to the old spider of the largest species. This one creature, "at the hour when sleep is at its deepest," slowly exits through its hole and "listens attentively for any rustling that may stir its mandibles in the air. Considering its insect's conformation it cannot do less ... than attribute mandibles to rustling" (180). A detail that, in an ironic light, explains how the creative power of an obsessive motif acts and how this nighttime noise becomes the conscious hallucination of a figure of the night. The rustling preceded the mandibles, but the old spider, in order to have consciously come out of the depths of this noise, is only more real because its reality is not that of a simple insect: to its presence is associated the imperceptible "immensity" of sleep, the reminiscence of the anguish of the entire past, the suffocating sadness of a distant memory, guilt, which the slightest noise evokes, announcing, screamed by the voice of forgiveness, the bodyless name of the greatest friendship. All this is in the image of the rustling sheet of paper and all this, continuing to live, took the form of this sluggish subject of the black tarantula, the "immense suction" of which, during a night lasting ten years, stupefied Maldoror's "expiring will" and engendered a muddled series of nightmares and the tragic effort, having come from the very depths of the dream, in order to grasp and to overcome the dream.

The Final Revelation

Now all the elements of the work, heretofore becoming, come together. The timid vampirism of the rhinolophe became this endless sucking. The paralysis that momentarily prevented Lautréamont from writing is the overwhelming oppression of these ten years, this open wound at the base of his neck where, a significant detail and a final allusion to the mysterious vertebral fixation,[123] the spider has made his nest. And the spider itself is only the final metamorphosis of the dreadful woman, the one that carried within it, in the enormous dream that is *Maldoror*, the common image of a vague, anguished memory and of the oppression that this memory introduced into sleep. The bizarre excremental sphere, in which, led by the powerful dreamlike and erotic attraction of the image of the whirlwind, this fear had taken form, presently gave birth to the monstrous stomach of the spider; likewise the insignificant friction of the thighs of the beetle against the edges of its elytrae, a sign nonetheless of formidable fury (165–66), passed into the imperceptible rustling of the mandibles. Now—the nightmare at this moment reveals it—this monstrous stomach, as in a double-pouched sack, contains two adolescents, the fraternal couple of Reginald and Elseneur, who, in the end, dash forward from this inner refuge, in order to discover, through this two-fold virile form, the ambiguous meaning of the memory hidden behind the overwhelming anguish of the female figure. But we recognize these two adolescents, betrayed in the past one after the other by Maldoror. They are just the two brothers, both of them also betrayed by the woman of the black ball and changed by her—because she has, we are told, the magician's power—into a beetle and into a pelican.[124] The mythic power of the narration has in some way attracted them to the interior of the black ball, which has thus absorbed them, devoured them, before definitively returning them to the light of day. Finally, so that all the movements might here reach their appointed end, we uncover the strangely divided action, the one that, while the beetle and the pelican, fraternally united, were discussing the fate of their victim, one leaning toward pity, the other toward retaliation (the same sentiment here: Reginald would like to forgo revenge, Elseneur pushes him toward it), projected them into the sky, where, this time, they struggled one against the other, a struggle that the author, judging it absurd, brings to an end. Fabrications of a seemingly gratuitous imagination, which, presently, occur within a clear and ordered narration. Herein one sees how Reginald, at first treacherously struck by his dearest friend, Maldoror, then replaced within this friendship by Elseneur, who Maldoror also strikes, throws himself, according to traditional novels, into the war and into fighting where he meets, masked, precisely Elseneur with whom he alone struggles in combat, up to the moment when both of them recognize each other (like Maldoror and the drowned Holzer) and fall into each others' arms. "He and I," Elseneur says to Maldoror, "swore eternal friendship; but one certainly different from those first two in which you had been the chief actor!" (186).

Before this denouement, in the form of a story borrowed ironically from the most banal depths of novelistic folklore, we must remain attentive to this: in such a transformation behind which different images are reunited, having reached, as if by chance their point of common maturity, the work seems to want, for a short moment, to halt, in order to make itself visible under the guise of a uniquely coherent figure. But this figure has nothing in common with the final vision of ordinary works of literature, a vision that the reader, in well-written books, knows is waiting for him, whereas, in poorly written and constructed books, it merely seems expected. In canto V, a similarly clear image, wherein exceptional fears, figures of a past unlike no other, of tragically unique dreams, by their particular movement made to fit the most conventional plot, at first has no other meaning than to represent the ultimate moment of an enormous rise toward the light of day, of the dramatic struggle of the dream of waking and the fight of lucidity, freed at the very moment when it sees itself as a prisoner. In this ultimate moment, being one of transparency, it is natural that so many very obscure images only give birth to the tranquil daylight of a banal narration, disappear and vanish in it, because they only aspired to this daylight, and the entire work had only been their slow struggle to overcome their own obscurity and, through each transformation, using it, exhausting it, and, finally, changing it into this brightness of a pure transparency.

It is obvious that Lautréamont, in this final revelation, if he arrives from the other side of sleep, if he sees through it, at the same time manages to get a handle on a theme that up to now had always eluded him. Naturally the thin fabric of the narration, in what it manifests, divulges nothing more on this theme of the fraternal couple than what has been suggested so many times and, in what it conceals, always keeps hidden, by the ambiguous meaning of the images, even the underhanded, solitary, and secret event, which forever linked the idea of friendship to that of aggression. But, first, this secret is always more hunted, the figures talk more

and more, and the symmetrical repetition of the story of Reginald
and Elseneur has no other purpose than to symbolically reduce the
scope of this mystery. In Reginald's story, the aggression still main-
tains a character of deep dream-like reality. Maldoror and his
friend, both "expert divers," disappear within the "bosom of the
deep," and it is in the depths of this aqueous mass, at the heart of
which they are seemingly lost, that suddenly the event takes place,
an event forever hidden, a mystery that mixes (as in the stanza
about coupling with the female shark)[125] blood with water and
water with blood—and after this event that encompasses and
evokes the profound depths of the ocean, the "tragically negative
hunt" begins, Reginald pursuing his companion in vain (like the
child on the omnibus), calling him three times, "and thrice," the
narrator says, "you replied with a cry of delight" (183). What there-
fore is the secret? Only a "microscopic hole" appears on the right
side and, as a sharp-edged blade, as a stiletto with the sharpest
point would be, "alone could claim *parentage* of so neat a wound.
He, Reginald, would never relate the various phases of the plunge
into the bosom of the deep, and has kept the secret to this very
day ... : memory is sometimes more bitter than the event" (184).[126]
Certainly herein lies what is hidden. But, in this regard, what is
manifest is the character of this aggression, aggression in the midst
of the water, which brings together, in a privileged way, both kinds
of images, which in the entire work served to give this idea of
aggression an erotic meaning[127]: the attack with the help of a
stiletto with the sharpest point, but the staggering crime, carried
out within the turbulent mass of the water and receiving from this
mass all of what is evoked by the two-fold image of the sea and the
whirlwind. With the second episode, Elseneur's, we truly reach the
edge of wakefulness: the attack is done for all to see. Maldoror
beats down on his friend "as the hurricane blows down the aspen
leaf;" the knife, now, is visible, it is even at the point of only being
disguised by irony, "draw[n], says the victim, from the sheath
hanging from your belt" (185). And, still, one last time, the solitary
aggression ends in failure: Maldoror, being unable to overcome his
adversary, "contented [himself] with cutting through my right

wrist, giving a quick flick of the steel blade" (186)—a detail perfectly chosen to bewitch the "psychoanalytic" analysis, since everything happens as if the missing act, in Maldoror's getting his revenge for his failure with a characteristic mutilation, is meant to shift the fatality of failure onto guilty childhood behaviors.

Now, the recognition of the two adolescents, Reginald and Elseneur (after unproductive fighting wherein the image of the whirlwind became "the cyclone of death"), and the eternal friendship that they swore to each other, are the last transformation of the dream that can only enter into the light of day purified and rendered sublime,[128] but if this purity is at the price of daylight and the sign of deliverance, it is what allows itself to be read in the resigned consent of the discourse to this conclusion, which marks its exhaustion. Each time, it is truly necessary to see that the conclusion is itself only possible because, with it, sleep comes to an end. It is not because feelings become pure and clear that the awakening happens, but this purity and clarity is the very opening up of the day that arises. True "deliverance" comes, in fact, from this final discovery of the work, which, in the deep bewitching image of the black tarantula, the center of which encircles all the obsessions of the now dead past, succeeded in making the dreamer accept the consciousness of his sleep and making him recognize within this paralyzing sleep and in this fear of a still not clearly grasped event the two faces of the same torment. Up to the last moment, just as the secret resists, so the dreamer tries to save a bit of what seems to him to be his free will. Admirable agony, tenacious fighting to the end. We have seen throughout that, in the most complete inertia, in the despondency of metamorphosis, in the putrefaction of death, Lautréamont is always affirming the permanence of his sovereignty. And here the apparition of the old spider no doubt marks first, for the hero, a surprise, the surprised feeling of his powerlessness. The "I who make sleep and nightmares recoil" suddenly finds itself completely paralyzed. "Remarkable thing!" But soon he pulls himself together, he struggles inch by inch, he announces that he is going to wake up in a sudden burst "through a last effort of my expiring will." Even more: he tries to reestablish his rights over the charm that makes him a prisoner while claiming to consent freely to it: "Yet I vaguely recall having given you permission to let your legs swarm over my blossoming breast." A vain trick that we recognize: it is that of lucidity that falls asleep because it refuses to sleep, but, "mesmerized meaning," "in the midst of the profoundest sleep," "reasons" always "supported by an incomparable subtlety, admirably." And, to better mark that the illusion of this last sudden burst is not returned only to what happens in this moment, in other words to the actual spider episode, but, through it, to every preceding experience in *Maldoror*, which is thus identified with the conflict of a long nightmare, the scene appears to us for the first time in the dreamer's thoughts, the dreamer who is receiving his dream, recounting it, remembering it, before beginning again to live it. But now, Lautréamont says, "we are no longer in the narrative ... Alas! We have ... reached the real," and the impression is in fact one of so many nightmares wherein the dreamer dreams that his dream shatters and opens onto truth. And the torture begins again. The resolution to not sleep yields to the secret decision that such a resolution envelops: this fatal "promise" by the will that had also been incriminated. The night again becomes the enormous suction-cup. "Death," the sleeper asks. Well, what happens? Is this death, is this life? Darkness clears, the spider's stomach opens up revealing what was hidden therein, and as the image embodying an unbearable daydream, if it opens up, loses principally its energy or its agonizing force, this vision of what the dream hides dissipates its enchantment, and Maldoror awakes to this ultimate revelation: that he himself was connected to his torment by proudly believing he was making himself free of it; he has not stopped submitting to an irrevocable decree. "Awake, Maldoror! ... you are free ."

The End of Experience, the Beginning of the Novel

H. R. Linder, within this text, means to impart an echo of Revelations: Maldoror, imprisoned within the ten-year-long night, is Satan, projected into the abyss and burdened by chains for a thousand years. The preceding stories in *Maldoror* would only be dreams of this Satan, thus connected to the abyss and looking to imagine his story, his revolt against God, his fall and his captivity. After a thousand years, the angel comes, frees him, but since this deliverance takes place today, it is because of us that Satan, freed once more to disrupt the world, flies into a rage; it is on the streets of Paris, modern-day Babylon, that we encounter him in the course of canto VI, and the story of his misdeeds is no longer that of the dream of the abyss, but, conforming to universal time, it unfolds in a logical way and according to a regular plot line. All of our unhappiness, for Ducasse, would come from this: our epoch is only the last episode of the satanic struggle wherein evil definitely took possession of the world.

After all! If the interpretation gives rise to doubt, at least it opens up a perspective on Maldoror that is equal to it. But Linder has not seen that his hypothesis supposes this condition: that Ducasse really has been or believed himself to be the great Satan of Revelations; because, if *Maldoror* is truly a dream of an abyss, this abyss is firstly Lautréamont's, and the stories do not form a simple lyrical, mystical meditation without any connection to their author; they also concern his existence, and it is the torment of this existence and the depths of his peculiar past that they try to bring to the light of day through the extended effort of a narration at the heart of which the images, the imaginary powers and the real memories of life, take shape, are developed, feel their energy, then, through each metamorphosis, having discovered the fundament of obscure things, in this obscure *discovered* fundament, they attain the deliverance of daylight. It is enough, truthfully, when we read *Maldoror*, to be passive about this movement of images, to their course and to their transformations, to recognize, within this disordered procession and in this capricious tumult of words, the most obstinate work and the most extraordinarily pursued experience that exists: one of a work persuaded to attain, in isolation from logical unity, a coherence however absolute and, this coherence achieved, to make it equally the greatest clarity and the greatest obscurity, the lowest *point*, the furthest from lucidity and the moment wherein lucidity, penetrating this point, is again found and liberated. And, no doubt, the world of *Maldoror* is often a mythical world, and the events that are therein sketched make the characters clash excessively with the apparent humanity of Isidore Ducasse; but, surely, Ducasse's real experience includes these mythical events—in the insane tension of the relationship with God, in the abrupt metamorphosis into a swine, in the gradual conspiracy with the octopus, as in Maldoror's satanic fiction, we find the equivalent of these excessive forces that rip him apart, but that he never stops wanting to reconquer freely and on behalf of this freedom.

Linder's interpretation rests on a just observation: the end of canto V marks, in the work, a turning point, and even its actual denouement. Commentators have at times noticed this, and Lautréamont, always completely conscious, commented in his own way on this change, which appears to him so radical, between what he has already written and what he is going to write. He does not see any more of a connection than between a preface and a novel, between the foundation of an edifice and the edifice itself. A revealing comparison. As in a work of foundation, it is truly in the depths of the earth that the work of *Maldoror* has up to now taken place: a gradual and persevering thrust toward the surface, the gigantic work of a buried man who, gradually, rose up, was enlightened, and now appears in the daylight, ready to act in the world. When Lautréamont talks about previous pages as about a "preceding observation" and about a "synthesis" (189), nothing more meaningful: he explained himself, he dragged himself into the light, and this explanation consisted in this convergent movement by which the disordered elements of his profound anterior obscurity learned how to be affirmed together. Now, he says of the story that is about to follow, "I am going to fabricate a novel" (190) and in fact the story that comes will no longer be related to him directly, it is a story that receives the character and the slightly gratuitous nature of fiction; but in contrast, we truly see how "the first five narrations" (189) touch his most personal reality, not only because they have uncovered the oppression that the old world inflicted on him, preventing him from living, but because they helped him get out of this "cavernous" (190) existence and prepared him to rage in today's world.

Everything happens precisely as if Ducasse had the feeling that, in relation to the *novels* that he is proposing to write, the previously written work manifested the necessary effort toward the progressive birth of the *novelist*: through this work, the absent Being that *Lautréamont* is slowly struggles, truly representing the hard work of birth, in this flowing of blood, of frames of mind, in this collaboration of patience and violence that birth is, Lautréamont, definitively pushing Ducasse aside, brought himself into the world; now, he exists, the novelist exists, and it seems to him that he has from the beginning had in hand all of what is necessary to write a good number of novels, "a series," beginning with maybe five or six.

Undoubtedly, when we read canto VI, what astounds us first is its quality of clear and orderly narration: the events follow one another, the plot is well established, the characters act, and all this for all to see, in the order of a composition of which the writer is master. But no less remarkable is the inner clarity of the work, the momentum, the magnificent speed with which everything follows everything, everything bursts apart. The acts, which no obstacle stops, take place in an admirably daring fury. There is no longer any struggle and there is no longer any time. The metamorphoses come to fruition on time. The battle with God is nothing more than the opportunity for an activity performed in the joy and drunkenness of unequaled vitality. It is to this part of *Maldoror*, and solely herein, that Gaston Bachelard's remarks on the intensity of Lautréamont's agile imagination, on the nature of time, the time of action, of aggression, which tolerates no delay, when nothing is any longer passive, nothing is expected, when suffering is given, never received, apply.[129] An important change, the causes of which, for us, are clear. It is that, precisely with canto V, sleep comes to an end; it was necessary for Lautréamont to have this enormous pain, this tragic experience of five cantos to liquidate the passive powers, the paralysis that stopped his pen, the stupor that immobilized him and that he desperately attempted to overcome, through trickery, methodically making it his own, while substituting for it this sovereign passivity of which he left us such proof. Certainly, in the five cantos, as we observed, the climactic moment is not lacking, nor is frenzy, nor outbursts of the stormiest passions. But this is precisely *Maldoror*'s deep-seated characteristic: this frenzy is also sleep, this climactic moment is immobility, this outburst stupor, sleeping life (violence and the depth of the ocean); and, these two extremes being those of desire, the tension when they bring resolute Being to live them to the fullest, in their simultaneous excesses, raises it or makes it fall outside its limits, in this experience of metamorphosis, sometimes wanted, sometimes anxiously withstood, and so close to the erotic experience wherein it truly is visible, wherein the most intoxicated, violent shifts result in a substantial collapse, of the mysterious transformation into the depths of another reality.

Lautréamont, in his prologue, told us, "the nightmares placed too much above ordinary existence" (189) are finished. And this dismissal is not a caprice. There are no longer any nightmares: evaporated in the daylight, they are one with him, they have become his clear and visible substance, so much so that, for a moment, we are going to see them once again, but no longer from within, from without, in their own form, in the clear vision of an appearance deprived absolutely of shadow and such as the day can carry it, show it, with all the energy that an imagination freed of its heavy particles gives. Hence, during the entirety of canto VI, the pursuit of the theme of metamorphosis; then also the facility, the ease of this narration, that of the dream-like life seems to only conserve the soaring, the flight forever eluding the anguish of the fall. Prodigious ease, which has its price: first, and naturally, Lautréamont returns to the plan as the beginning of the work, unaware that it was going to become an experience, searching for a literary framework. Maldoror therefore recommences his role as corrupter, and also as vampire, which he then preferred to become; he presently basks, with complete lucidity, in the powerful jubilance of his Luciferian role. It is also that the image of the vampire, with his double life, with the anguish that accompanies him, would no longer agree with the boundless power of the new Maldoror, who, additionally, so as to exert his unlimited might, truly needs the entire expanse of land and sky and the obliging adversary that is his match, Elohim. This turning backward is characterized by the recommencement of the same scenes, the family picture at the beginning becomes the point of departure for all of canto VI, but this return to the novel also entails a new and much more significant change: the tone changes, the irony becomes something different.

Irony and Metamorphosis

We are sure, through the entire course of the work, irony played a supreme role, and, as in no other work, we are unable to uncover anything analogous to it. It was *the scalpel that pokes fun, these anathemas, possessors of the talent for provoking laughter,* both sides of the cutting edge of negativity, one its clear, lucid side, the other buried in the depths of the wound. Schopenhauer wrote that humor was the only truly divine quality, the only one that made us free.[130] But this placid remark, rather stripped of humor, hardly makes its exorbitant force felt. On the contrary, Lautréamont, when he says God has generally not exceeded the ordinary laws of the grotesque (speaking in this way almost like the philosopher), soon registers, in the glint of sarcasm, the very shift of sarcastic power, that of eternal laughter, which turns all things on their head, even itself, an overturning so extensive and pushed to such a point of instability that, through it, every standard is exceeded, even the transcendent dimension that is God. *Irony,* the entirety of *Maldoror* testifies, *is the very experience of the metamorphosis sought at the heart of language,* lucidity attempting to lose itself in order to seize itself, the tremor of reason having become "cadaverous," meaning forever in flight to become the reality of nonsense; and, if *Maldoror,* alone perhaps in the entirety of literature, can give this impression of an immense, full, compact and solid existence, it is that the prodigious power of irony brought very close to words the possibility of metamorphosis to which they contribute, which they help complete, all while rendering it dangerously conscious of itself (because within this consciousness, conscience or metamorphosis risks being lost), and this impending change, that words would no longer be words, or the things that they mean, or this meaning, but something *else*, a thing forever different, is rather insistent, so that reading *Maldoror* is, due to the wait, the suspense, already experiencing this change.

In canto VI, the irony remains all-powerful, but, in this distinct world, with no darkness and no sleep, it softens into parody. Having become a novel, *Maldoror* strives, through irony, to become a parody of the novel and, in particular, of the popular novel. The intention to mock is clear at every moment: a parody of mysterious action-packed plots, of unbelievable and barely justified dramatic turns; a caricature of certain stock characters, belonging obligatorily to the Anglo-Saxon aristocracy, always inhabiting luxurious residences and expressing themselves in a ridiculously formal language; a game, finally, that distracts itself, obligingly insists on the lack of seriousness of the fiction and turns everything into mockery, beginning with Maldoror.[131]

Assuredly, this informality is a great pleasure, and Lautréamont's virtuosity without fault. But the parody is unable to progress beyond itself and, in exerting its sovereignty over only the pleasant extravagances of the popular novel, it further distances itself "from the infamous voluptuousness of an irony, turned killjoy, that exceeds the accuracy of thought," and even more from "the guilt of a writer who rolls down the slope of nothingness and scorns himself with joyful cries" (214–15). (Ducasse, apparently wanting, in the *Poésies*, to make the malefic power of sarcasm felt, puts forth these formulations that especially make clear the meaning and the aim of his own irony.)

We are beginning to see it: it is the reigning law that is affirmed. Even the images, in their fabulous speed, become more distinct and more precise. The acts are pure. The struggle with the Almighty, turned into a rhinoceros, is hunting without a trap, a struggle without spasm: nothing more distinct than a cone-shaped bullet that riddles the skin of the pachyderm. Another sign: the eroticism withdraws. Neither around the figures, nor around the action, is the halo of sexual dread seen, though it had been visible throughout the entire work. The episode with Mervyn, though connected to all the fatalities of fraternal love, gives rise only to insignificant desires and to the sadism of illusion.[132] Ducasse no longer participates. As if here were being entertained and from afar, he calmly witnesses the admirable proceedings of his ironic imagination. At certain moments, we are even under the impression that this so very exacting story line bores him. Then he returns to the "synthetic section," he hears the faint murmur of old obsessions—an obsession for ugliness, for the mirror, for the eye, in the stanza inspired by Edgar Allen Poe[133]—and this return, which interrupts the flow of the novel, is like an attempt at dread in order to escape the demands of a highly objective form. Likewise, the episode with Aghone and the three Marguerites, when once again erotic memories are insinuated, expresses one last time the collusion that Lautréamont would like to prolong with the "inaccessible places," his nostalgia for an original intimacy, now shattered. The figure of Aghone, a fool with moments of intermittent madness, is a memory, but one that already parodies the past: and "the alabaster crown," a symbol of power with which Maldoror coifs him, all while undoubtedly referencing the oldest adolescent images—retains no more than a derisive glimmer of these images.[134]

The Apotheosis of an Image

Certain commentators have deemed the end of the sixth canto as lacking anything that might make it the true end of *Maldoror*. This might be possible. However, it might also be possible that the end, in such a work, was necessarily destined to leave us, instead, with an impression of the infinite. And yet we must not neglect the obvious care with which Lautréamont labored over the final image, an image of apotheosis, which is also, we said, the apotheosis of an image, one whose substance, continuously transformed, sustained *Maldoror* from beginning to end—and whose three great phases were the image of the hair, the image of the whirlwind, and the image of the meteor, the image itself linked to that of the look that could kill, and that of the nocturnal light of blood.[135] Mervyn's parabolic flight, which Lautréamont calls "the one damned to death," and which in the end carries him off, his hands rigid, gripping the deathless flowers, up to the dome of the Pantheon, a place where death is glorious, assuredly represents Maldoror's final flight. And this admirable triumph, which makes him "resemble a comet with its flaming tail trailing after it" (218), all while rendering him immortal, in the end only leads to a dried-up skeleton, confirming the final and important meaning of a figure composed with so much attention. A monumental, and nearly too perfect image, whose calculated form, in accordance with the commandments of an exacting reason, serves so to speak as a symbol for this new sovereignty of light, which had already been called, though by an act of faith and a still irrational sermon, the first hymn to mathematics. Mervyn's apotheosis, which ushers him into glory and into death, is therefore also the apotheosis of the light of day, and the denouement of the sixth canto is, from here, only the denouement of the fifth canto repeated all over again, with the difference that the light, at that earlier moment, was only the break of day, while presently, and with a surprising pace, the promises of the day find their realization, which is that the poetic imagination, in the glory and ease of daylight, perhaps also finds its realization and its death, like a slowly dissipating radiance.

The impression remains that, with this image and this apotheosis, Lautréamont has truly arrived at the end of the cantos, though this swift end surprised him, and would have at least surprised the Lautréamont full of hope and of gay force who, beginning canto VI, promised himself to write, not one, but several, perhaps five, six novels or episodes in the genre used for Mervyn (which would have brought the cantos to twelve). We can say to ourselves that, when Lautréamont, speaking of "the series of instructive poems I am longing to produce" (190), writes, "Dramatic episodes of a relentless utility!" (190), or even, "Today, I am going to fabricate a little novel of thirty pages; this amount will subsequently remain more or less fixed" (190), and, "only later, when a few novels have come out, will you better understand the preface of the renegade with the dusky face" (190), within these perspectives there is plenty of irony for us not to take them more seriously than the author himself does. Undoubtedly. However, Lautréamont never writes without reason: as light as they want to be, his words are not written lightly, and when he announces something (that such and such a detail will be clarified, such and such an event is going to happen), subsequently, always, with an ironic bent, he keeps his promises. It is therefore probable that, liberated from himself, seeing the range of an activity that seems to him limitless extend before him, when he obligingly draws up this grand writing program, his intentions respond well to what he shows us: for him, then, and truly, he puts off, until much later, the end of his work, which appears to him capable of sustaining itself over a long run. After a few pages, the end looms imminently; soon it is here and the end of this lone "novel" makes the project of all the others disappear. Why? What happened? Hans Rudolf Linder says he was caught unprepared by the publication deadline: he would not have had enough time. Time? Not at this particular time, but rather the internal time of the work, and the work itself. It is the work that is lacking, having achieved in this light what it intended to achieve, after having achieved which the work had nothing more to say that was truly important to him.

Completion

Everything happens as if *Maldoror*, finished as an experience with canto V, was unable to prolong itself any longer as a work of literature and of normal fiction. Everything gives the impression that *Maldoror*, after having confirmed the birth of the novelist and his total mastery, his definitive viability, had, in every sense of the word, liberated him from himself, such that he himself dematerialized as much as he was materialized and, once in possession of all his faculties, he lost use of them, having neither the taste for nor perhaps the possibility of continuing a task that risked becoming a game, and a game too distinct to even be in accordance with the original intention of *Maldoror* (connected to the problem of evil). It is perhaps significant that, at the end of canto V, seeing himself freed from the intolerable nightmare of so very long a night, then witnessing the break of day, Maldoror, at this moment, really far from the magnificent joy that always sustained him even in the midst of the most tragic metamorphoses, experiences only a devastated feeling, a feeling of having only achieved a pathetic life, a dawn that is already twilight, when the relief that welcomes him dooms him to the boredom of a henceforth already certain existence.[136] And no doubt within this sadness there is the feeling that deliverance is the inverse of his past servitude (similarly what is peculiar to absolution is making the memory of the crime unerasable)—and also that this deliverance demanded his complete abdication, the recognition of the "irrevocable decree" to which he submitted every time that he believed he was liberated from it. But justifiably, it is truly to a true abdication, to an act of self-renunciation, to his happy past, to his torments, and, finally, to the common origin of his weakness and his strength that he had to subscribe. The apathy that grips Maldoror is really one that seizes every "healed" or freed man, when, freed from excess and from revolt, he sees himself given over to the resignation of a miserly or deficient wisdom. This is why, too, the last stanza of the work—which would confirm that, at this moment, Lautréamont is really ready to finish it—in the famous passage wherein he wonders if he truly succeeded in cretinizing the reader, reveals, with the prospect of his impending death, the feeling that this death will consist first and foremost in the abandonment of his task, in the impossibility, perhaps, of continuing his sleepwalking magnetism, this experience of obscuring with a light that is now no longer a self-imposed test but a simple method, in addition to its rich prospects, of literary provocation. His epitaph therefore truly sheds "light," like a last and final defiance, on the power that allowed him to humiliate this light; but the defiance is engraved, symbolically, on a tomb, as if there were no longer any other place from which to launch his provocation than from the tomb, which remains his last accomplice and the only future for his hope.[137]

"Poésies"

We have often wondered about the little book entitled *Poésies* and about the lines that shape its epigraph: "I replace melancholy with courage, doubt with certainty, despair with hope, wickedness with goodness, complaints with duty, skepticism with faith, sophisms with the indifference of calm, and arrogance with modesty" (223). Is this a denial from the bottom of his heart? A simple literary about-face, provoked by the difficult publication of *Maldoror*, which was threatened by the police and unsuccessful? A mystifying enterprise wherein an apology for the good is only a sarcastic way, in these dangerous times, of continuing to promote evil? Or really and resolutely has he henceforth switched sides, to the side of order? *Poésies*, "preface" (those too) "to a future book," are remarkably ambiguous and much less adamant than the few letters wherein he protests his good sentiments. A great number of "thoughts,"[138] if they celebrate virtue, celebrate it disdainfully, or on the contrary with an excessiveness so extreme that praise becomes defamation. Attributing Villemain with thirty-four times more intelligence than Sue, placing a second-rate professor over Dumas and Balzac, recognizing in discussions of the distributions of prizes the only masterworks in our language, such is his standard when he defends standards and his seriousness in service of seriousness.

Does he ask that we be polite with the creator, with such irreverence in this concern for politeness, such disdain! "Do not display bad taste and a breach of the most basic proprieties toward the creator ... Repel disbelief: you'd be doing me a favor" (223). What insolence in the contradictory postulations of his new optimism: "Man is perfect ... Progress exists" (235). In *Paul et Virginie*, a masterpiece of benevolence, he sees the most horrible of black books: "In the past, this episode, which broods gloomily from the first to the last, especially the final shipwreck, made me gnash my teeth. I would roll upon the carpet and kick my wooden horse" (231). On Victor Hugo: "Nothing will remain but his poems about children; there's much that is bad" (231). Certainly, he affirms that God's wisdom is admirable; but "misfortune becomes august through the impenetrable will of God who created it" (231). Or even: "Misfortune ... is in Elohim" (248). On God, his thoughts remain, besides, very "bad": "The principle of worship is pride. It is ridiculous to address Elohim ... Praying is a false act" (238). "Elohim is made in the image of man" (244). "I allow no one, not even Elohim, to doubt my sincerity" (236), truly a very strange way to combat doubt.

It is in *Poésies* that he defines, on the pretext of condemning it, the romantic aesthetic, and defines himself through the most impartial of formulations, with a penetration and a freedom of judgment that shows just how close the spirit of this literature still is to him. With such mastery he keeps it at a distance, to better see it, and to see how he knows himself, as he was, as he undoubtedly no longer wants to be—either he dismisses "the hallucinations waited upon by the will, ... deep-thinking imaginations, ... precocious and abortive experiences, obscurities with a flea-like shell, ... inoculation with deep stupors, ... rational terrors, ... neuroses, the cruel routes through which one forces last-ditch logic, exaggerations, lack of sincerity" (224), in other words, all of what makes the mistake of transforming a distraction into a method. Or he describes "the foul mass graves": "frogs, octopi, sharks, the simoom in the deserts, whatever is clairvoyant, squinting, nocturnal, narcotic, somnambulist, slimy, ... whatever is thoughtless as a child, desolation, that intellectual manchineel tree, perfumed chancres, thighs like camellias, the guilt of a writer who rolls down the slope of nothingness and scorns himself with joyous cries,[139] remorse, hypocrisies, the vague perspectives that grind you within their imperceptible mills" (224). Or he even imagines what hides behind the appearance of writers like him: "Picture them for a moment reunited in society with substances that would be their counterparts. It is an uninterrupted succession of combats undreamed of by bulldogs, forbidden in France, by sharks and the macrocephalic cachalots. These are torrents of blood, in these chaotic regions full of hydras and minotaur, and whence the dove, frightened off forever, flies swiftly away. There is a mass of apocalyptic beasts who are not unaware of what they do. These are collisions of passions, irreconcilabilities and ambitions, through the shrieks of an indecipherable pride that controls itself and whose reefs and depths none can, not even approximately, fathom" (228).

Such a text leaves no room to doubt the sincerity of Lautréamont's critical passions, no less so the collusion that, perhaps despite himself, the violence into which these passions lead him re-establishes with all that he condemns. This contradiction is not new. In the past, during the time of "filthy mass graves," what he loved he sometimes loved too much, and then hated, ripped apart; and what he did not love, he abhorred, and the abhorrence opened him up to desire. The metamorphosis, this attempt to enter "society with substances that were his likeness," thereby precipitated, much more that sympathy, the anguish of the disgust; and when he inflicted pain, he did it, sometimes through excessive pity, sometimes through remorse, most often in a breathtaking spirit of revolt, and sometimes a methodical uneasiness, which drove him to always behave worse, as if to hurt himself and, within this immeasurable instability, to find a solution to this evilness and a new horizon of freedom (which at this particular time, evidently, was clearly not the good).

At no time was evil a simple theoretical idol for him. One could say that the "evil" was in him, and, quite nearly, was him. This evil not relinquishing him, he put up an admirable fight, and since he found nothing in himself that was evil, except for the consciousness that he had of it, a sovereign power that he marvelously assured, he was only able to combat evil with evil, making himself its accomplice and pushing it as far as possible, in the steadfast— but also spellbound—courage of his resolution and in the hope of a radical overtaking, which might return him to himself or throw him outside everything. If, now, he preaches order, reason, we cannot therefore say that he disowns his past convictions, because his tragic fight was a fight for daylight, and he always wanted to see clearly. In this sense, he remains perfectly faithful to himself and, as he says in a letter, "it is always, therefore, the good one who sings, in short" (258). But it is also really true that between yesterday and today the change risks being great: keeping his eyes open when darkness is sovereign and easily taking pleasure in reasonable tranquil clarity, the man who moves from the first attitude to the second is no longer the same man; and he changes much more since, judging himself more changed than he is, when he turns toward a past that he rejects, he does not want to acknowledge anything more within this past struggle, in the middle of the night, than an unhealthy excessive indulgence for the night, in this brooding will nothing but a weakness, a game and an experience both lacking sincerity and value.

Writing, Dying

From *Maldoror* to the *Poésies*, there is both a continuity and a rupture, but the rupture is already announced by *Maldoror*: its denouement is outside and infinitely separated from itself, which it shows us through a perspective of death on which it closes with a rather lugubrious resignation. From the *Poésies*, finally, two impressions are extracted. When Lautréamont places the analysis of feelings over feelings themselves, and when he prefers to all others the writer who does not let himself be betrayed by his passions or by himself, when he tries to reconcile poetic enthusiasm and the composure of the moralist, when he writes, "Judgments on poetry are of more value than poetry" (242), this praise of clarity, this completely Valérian preference for extreme consciousness in poetry and for poetic consciousness, all these steadfastly reasonable affirmations already supposed by the first cantos of *Maldoror*, where the voice of mathematics alternates with that of the ocean, surprise much less when, freed by *Maldoror* and also from *Maldoror*, Lautréamont, having settled his score with the dark forces and erased "the childish reversal of things," is condemned, through his very triumph, to the certainty of a uniquely positive reason (his hostility with regard to Elohim is a sign of this positive spirit). Through the *Poésies*, he therefore becomes precisely conscious of the situation, which is now his own, of the success of his experience and of the conditions of a viable existence. Only—and herein lies the other remarkable fact—this specific consciousness is still an excessive consciousness; his measured resignation is itself similarly excessive. This is so clear that we might believe it an exaggerated defensive reaction, a hasty concern for breaking with a still dangerous past. But things are perhaps less simple.

In the last letter, which is also the last text that we have by him, Ducasse expresses himself in the following way:

> Allow me to resume from a while earlier. I have had a book of poetry published by M. Lacroix (B. Montmartre, 15). But once it was printed he refused to let it appear, because life was painted therein in colors that were too bitter, and he feared the Attorney General. It was something in the genre of Byron's *Manfred* and Mickiewic's *Konrad,* but far more terrible, however. Publication cost 1,200 francs, of which I had already found 400. But the whole thing went down the drain. This made me open my eyes. I told myself that since the poetry of doubt (of today's volumes not 150 pages will remain) has reached such a point of gloomy despair and theoretical nastiness, it's therefore because it is radically false; and the reason is that *it discusses principles, and one must not discuss them*: it's more than unjust. The poetic moans of this century are only hideous sophistry. To sing of boredom, suffering, miseries, melancholies, death, darkness, the somber, etc., is wanting at all costs to look only at the puerile reverse of things. Lamartine, Hugo, Musset have voluntarily metamorphosed into sissies. These are the Great Soft Heads of our epoch. Always sniveling! This is why I have completely changed methods, to sing exclusively only of *hope, expectation, CALM, happiness, DUTY.* And thus I rejoin with the Corneilles and the Racines the chain of good sense and composure brusquely interrupted since the posers Voltaire and Jean-Jacques Rousseau. My book will not be finished for four or five months. But in the meanwhile, I would like to send my father the preface, consisting of sixty pages; published by Al. Lemerre. (261)[140]

"The whole thing went down the drain. That made me open my eyes." No one would be ready to believe that his book's literary failure alone was enough to make him consider it as "false."

But if one more closely examines the bewitchment of his thoughts. The failure of his work "opened my eyes." This event therefore seems to have been a jolt, after which the new state, the other choice, implied in the evolution of *Maldoror* (and implied as its truth), abruptly crystallized. It is upon this incident that he became conscious of himself as changed and, while no doubt changed as a result of this work, changed also by this work, rendered completely different from it. Before, he had, so to speak, not existed, shut up within the stupor of childhood; presently, he is really in the world. Also, since the publication, always a decisive moment when the work is definitively separated from its writer, leads to failure, he is, through this incident, even more tempted to see *Maldoror* not as the triumphant success that it guaranteed him, but as the part of himself that is defeated and condemned, and to dedicate all the conscious strength that he owes the text to rejecting it and to hastily distancing himself from it, a condemnation all the more sincere since this failure has a grave meaning for him. His book not only had no success, but it was not even able to see the light of day—"the whole thing went down the drain," too absolute a failure not to be real. That he owes this book the light of publication, he can do no more than forget, seeing it as incapable of coming to light and as close to nothingness as is necessary to take it to be nothing. When, he says—this is the meaning of his letter—that the part played by negation reaches the point of ruining the expression of this part, this position is radically unfounded, this way of fighting, which questions the principles without which the fighting is impossible, is unjustified. That, while writing *Maldoror*, the young Ducasse dreamt of the glory of masterwork, is evident. But he always wanted more: in this book, which was his most personal experiment, he also had the feeling of bringing its task to everyone and, even in his solitude, of delivering a fight in which he is not alone. This is why the defiance of this book, falling through before ever reaching the public, therefore truly making it nothing, as if destroyed by him, without the slightest concern for others, announces a serious failing that opened his eyes.

"This is," he says, "why I have completely changed methods" (261). This methodological change, by which he returns to a clear classical vision, is therefore seriously motivated. Imperious, prompt as usual, he only gives himself a few months to complete the new book, for which the previously written preface took the name *Poésies*. He has, at this new turn of events, exactly the same confidence and the same boldness as at the beginning of canto VI, wherein he perceived, as the novelist who had just emerged, hope arising from a long series of novels to be written. The true turn of events took place then, though, at the moment—he had not completely measured its amplitude—when he would see more clearly after "the failure," but he nonetheless deciphered all of its perspectives and was not mistaken, as he was mistaken when he promised such a long sequel to *Maldoror*. The book that he is announcing, consecrated "exclusively to hope, calm, happiness, duty," did this book, however destined for a glory satisfied by the light of day, ever see the light of day? Did he ever write it? And if death alone prevented him, is it not that he could do no more than die and that at the point when he was to write, he was already dead, dying a death so similar to life that it pulled him from the world without anyone being sure that he had left this life? The truth, in all this, lets itself be felt. He was completely faithful to the light, but this faithfulness demanded of him a more complete disappearance, a more radical conversion than what his *calm* book showed. Similarly, while he is writing the sixth canto of *Maldoror*, the canto teaches him that there will not be a seventh, and that the work is nearing its end; likewise, to write or to try to write his calm book, he became aware that no book will be possible any longer, that the end is closing in and that what he believes a book to be is his own end.

The Impossibility of Limits

Poésies clarifies this situation. When, following the failure of *Maldoror*, Lautréamont condemns his excessive attempt as false and childish, when he attributes his failure to such excess, he understands that the struggle now consists in accepting limits, in renouncing the limitless will that drove him to God's level. But what is happening? A strange dilemma. The solution of the simple life, of the straight and narrow path and of the limited task, which he now welcomes as the truth of his renewed existence, is itself not simple. Everyone understands: at a precise moment, three years before Rimbaud, after an experience at once analogous and very different to his (because, driven entirely throughout a book wherein, however his life was from top to bottom put to the test, this experience, through its own movement, brought him to the point at which it was necessary for him to turn away from it, to reject it and to welcome the "extremely severe" meticulousness of "the new hour"), Lautréamont—after having spent an entirely similar season in hell, even characterized by erotic fear—is exactly at the "Adieu" that will throw Rimbaud into the desert of Harrar. But the same "Adieu" throws Lautréamont into a much gloomier desert, that of the good, and we see the difference. Likewise, Rimbaud's experience, in certain ways more methodical, more theoretical, and more deliberate—meanwhile engaging, as far as we presume, his life more—was just as much a lived adventure as an adventure of language; similarly the dismissal of the experience apparently only results in Rimbaud's life becoming, and shuts him up in this life like, a tomb. Lautréamont, who could only free himself from himself through the experience of a book, can free himself from this experience only with another book. He too invented "new flowers, new stars, new flesh, new languages," but when he "buries" all this, when he himself buries himself, it is still within the heart of literature. In principle, there is nothing very remarkable herein, and this way of going back on everything he once stood for can seem banal and not at all exemplary like Rimbaud. And each time such a banal denial, and even from some annoying, displeasing angle, in the end assumes the same mythical significance and gives way to a no less strange and no less fabulous enigma than what will glorify Rimbaud.

When Lautréamont begins writing the "Preface," he still seems to believe that, to conform to the rules of the "new hour," it is enough to "replace despair with hope, meanness with goodness," that is to say, in sum, to valiantly write a book wherein certainty is triumphant. An exalting project, a straight and narrow path wherein he arduously commits himself. But, even from his very first steps, the path begins to oscillate strangely, and soon it resembles—it is hard to tell them apart—the "abrupt and savage path" that the first words of *Maldoror* carved out. What therefore happens? With all the sincerity and imagination of which he is capable, he celebrates order. And all of a sudden this song of the glory of order becomes the raucous voice of chaos, rendering forever unusable the decent thoughts from which it borrows its appearance. What power is therefore in him, however turned toward the light, what creative overabundance, placed in vain in service of rules, but so great that it can only humiliate the rule and, behind it, glorify limitless freedom? Regardless of whether, sometimes, really, Lautréamont has a plan to render ridiculous what he praises, this is possible, but this intention is itself still only the unspoken sarcastic word that is the impetus and the seat of his reason. And from the moment this word speaks, with it the power of this reason bursts forth, more ample than all reason, and it pushes him bit by bit to the point of instability, wherein he must simultaneously express the meaning of what he is saying, and the inversion of this meaning, and the evolution of this inversion, in the plenitude of an unwavering ambiguity. Now if—up to a certain point—evil can make its *good* from what it denies, by the negation that it sees therein and with which it is in agreement, it is little otherwise than the good, and the excess that confirms the latter puts it more dangerously in peril than the measured contradiction wherein it could indirectly recognize itself. And yet, good, evil, here these are equivocal powers with which tricks are de rigueur. But at this moment, and in the mind of Lautréamont, it is a question of much more specific realities: of form, of language, and of the future even of what he must write. On this level, his convictions are from now on passions—passion for clarity, for lucid reason, *passion*, to reveal everything, *for composure*—that place him in absolute solidarity with what he affirms and what through the excessiveness of his passions and the nature and extent of his imagination soon transform into a trap wherein a completely contrary truth falls prey. In such an extremity, he is only able to win the day while fighting himself. Also the critical part of the *Poésies* is the most developed part, and the only one that holds out, because then he can legitimately take part in what he denies, being required to recognize it clearly; and, required to reject it vigorously, he can test all excessive violence against himself, all the strangeness of language for which he blames himself, a movement that has always been his own and led him to the deliverance of metamorphosis.

But does he want to praise "taste"? He praises Villemain, and with a disproportionate praise of the sort that, in the eyes of this tasteful writer, illuminates the mocking glow of nothingness, suddenly conscious and proud of its own void. Accepting limits is therefore not, for he who carries an infinite force within himself, a simple matter, a matter of *words*. Accepting limits? Yes, but first one must locate them. Whether or not one understands it, the excessive side of the *Poésies* comes from this excess that, in Lautréamont, is not a legacy of his senseless past, but the reason of his reason and the heart of his lucidity. Lucid he is, but being lucid is also being excessively lucid, is introducing, at the center of lucidity and as its principle, the risk of this excess, without which to see is to see nothing. In the present case, wherein it is in sum only a question of literature, what is at stake does not appear truly serious: it is just about "good" literature; the goal is to write well and, previously, to determine precisely the boundaries of this good. Lautréamont sets out in pursuit of these boundaries, interested more than anyone to find them, he who discerns in himself a dangerous longing for any limit, a seemingly easy pursuit that meanwhile leads him further than he thought, then even further. He must reject not only "filthy mass graves," not only the "devalued" writers—Sand, Balzac, Musset, Baudelaire—but Voltaire, Rousseau, then, later, Racine (no more tragedies), then Corneille, Boileau, Coppée. Crime novels, certainly, but *Paul et Virginie* also broods, and the *La Grève des Forgerons* (*Blacksmith's Strike*) and

Jocelyn.[141] Victor Hugo? From him we could perhaps keep some appropriate poems, like those about children—but on reflection, they have "much that is bad." Soon, there is nothing but Villemain, to whom, soon, one must prefer secondary school professors, who boast about not writing, then, finally, students in the fourth year of secondary school, more gifted in everything because they know nothing.[142]

It is possible that Lautréamont did not have a completely clear point of view—while still writing, it couldn't be—of the truth that haunts him, yet throughout the entire "Preface," this truth is looking for him: to know that writing well is impossible, because writing is always brooding, is being on the side of evil. He also attempts strange compromises: plagiarism, for example, the ultimate resource for he who, being unable to do without writing, does not however want to write; and if he imagines turning maxims upside down and, in particular, of rewriting a page of *Maldoror*, inverting its terms, it is that he is obsessed with the hope that the denial demanded by him will be able to be satisfied, if he replaces the word "melancholia" with the word "courage," the word "evil" with the word "good." It is this that he initially hoped for, and it is this that he despairingly attempts before this formidable flight from the limits that, if he advances in order to hang on to them, become evasive and carry him away. As for the inverted maxims, Cleopatra's nose having become world morality, this is again too much.[143] To attribute, he says, to the good what is said of evil, is dangerous. How far then to go? Silence? But the goal is to write, and silence is as vague as sleep, and we are seeking clarity, we want to be clear, unassuming, and modest as the day. While writing the preface, Lautréamont begins to sense which renunciation demands his loyalty to the light of day: not a renunciation resting on the meaning of words or on words alone, but a veritable negation, a self-destruction, a sacrifice of his entire person in order to rejoin, glorify and assure the cold movement of impersonal reason. In the final pages, the temptation becomes obvious: the appeal of daylight is made more forcefully. The famous expression, *Poetry must be made by everyone. Not by only one* (244), does not have a mysterious meaning: like the other thoughts that accompany it, it proposes raising poetry to a veritable science of maxims; poetry dreams of this wisdom of nations, which is the supreme point to which it aspires; it would like to be united with the supreme banality wherein (again like Valéry) it finds more genius than in any genius;[144] it searches for the path that would lead it to the common source of every science, of every logic,[145] to the impersonal principle that animates the theorem and wherein it hopes to recover the pure mockery of all indecency.[146]

Lautréamont and Hölderlin

Meaning and grandeur are easily perceived through such a temptation. In the movement, which is nonetheless that of immanence, in this quest for light, equal in all its points, the same for all, and wherein, all being reconciled, "all" is for each one the truth of which "each one" would be the complete appearance, Lautréamont again tries to grasp the infinite reality of a transcendence that he has never separated from himself and of which he made himself just as much an accomplice as an adversary. It is this infinite demand that led him to be at his lowest (which was also his highest), in terms of a metamorphosis wherein the limits of his person and the chains of human reality are shattered, and it is equally this metamorphosis that drives him, presently, toward another metamorphosis, that of absolute banality, wherein this time the acceptance of the limit will be the unlimited, and the moment representing the extreme point of consciousness, of reason, and of sovereignty will coincide with the abandonment of all personal sovereignty and consciousness. Thus falls on the poet, like the guillotine's blade, the terrible *tics, tics, and tics* by which poetry, with one word alone, reduces the originality of every singular existence to the nonentity of a maniacal aberration.[147] It is impressive to see how, in two beings as different in every way as Lautréamont and Hölderlin, the poetic experience, which seems to separate them still more, is manifested through the same profound vertigo, the same temptation, the same desire, that to attain this moment of light wherein, united with the light of day, each one will also be united with himself, with the intimacy of his own sunlit nature, while lost and saved within this burst of sunlight, which is like the infinite radiance of the nature of every being eager to dissipate into everything. If their destinies differed, it is perhaps that Hölderlin, seeing this moment within daybreak, attracted by this beginning, by this dawning of the day that appeared to him like his own beginning, gave way to the nostalgia of childhood and of the originary space, wherein, in finding himself again, he was able to hope to find death and life. But having loved light above all, and the nostalgia of his own beginning having never been a weak and personal desire, but firstly the purest passion, desire proud to be united with bright gods, it so happened that he was truly and absolutely united with the light to which he had the strength to sacrifice all his forces and that, in return, brought him this unique glory of a child's reasoning wherein all the splendor of impersonal clarity shined forth.

Lautréamont was unable to disappear within madness, being born of madness, nor into childhood, the force of light within him having rendered him more powerful than the madness and the nostalgia of childhood. Turning back to the past is not possible for he who has already withstood the experience of the return, has overcome it and, in this effort, really begun. Lautréamont is this strange being who, still unreal under the apparent name of Ducasse, wanted to give himself the light of day and to completely take on the responsibility of his own beginning. An attempt that is the truth of his myth. But, to he who wants to become master of his origin, it soon seems that being born is an infinite event. Being born is coming into daylight and, then, in the light of day looking for one's limits, without which there is no true being. And, limits being unable to be imposed from without, at the risk of destroying the right and responsibility of birth, they must be the very limit of the day, of this day that is already in Lautréamont an unlimited aspiration, which the extreme moment designates the sole, ideal, and real point at which, ceasing being himself, he can become, outside of himself, completely himself, in the end coming forever into the world at the ultimate moment that makes him disappear from it.

We know nothing about Ducasse's last moments. They were unable to be known, only able to appear in the ignorance that reveals its only truth. How did these last few hours unfold? Was the law, supreme incarnation of all-encompassing reason, in the farcical way of Napoleonic authority, directed against him? Did he himself, in a last move of his sovereignty, break the promise, made to *Maldoror*, to never attempt suicide, a promise that at this moment had meaning, because suicide was then the temptation of darkness, though today it is the temptation of light, and who would want to resist such an appeal of daylight? And yet he who, from one end to the other, associated his destiny with literature, who had already sought, through plagiarism, to disappear into the words of another, now, in the room on the fifth floor where formerly his still absent hand had succeeded in writing the "May it please heaven" that marked Maldoror's beginning as well as his own, in this same room where this time there is no longer any rustling or darkness or anguish or fear, before this, always *future*, book consecrated to tranquillity, understanding the meaning of this calm that, in order to take reality into words, demands to become the only substance of his life, does he know, in the furthest extremes of his lucidity, his final and only true metamorphosis, what at this moment changes him into modesty and tranquillity itself?

Lautréamont's end retains something of the unreal. Attested by the word alone of the law and in the brief mention of the act of death, "deceased … without other information," as reprimanded as possible by banality, it seems that this banality is lacking, not being needed to reach fruition. It is through his so strangely erased end that Lautréamont became, forever, this invisible way of appearing that is his figure alone, and is in the incognito of the death that he had, before everyone's eyes, shown himself to be, as if, in disappearing within such a radiant absence, he had perhaps found death, but also, in death, the just moment and the truth of the day.

Notes

What Is Criticism?

1. "In order that what has been purely written of in the poem may stand forth a little clearer, the explanatory speech must break up each time both itself and what it is has attempted. The final, but, at the same time, the most difficult step of every exposition consists in its own vanishing away together with its explanations in the face of the pure existence of the poem. The poem, which then stands in its own right, will itself throw light directly on other poems; we feel that we had always understood them in this way. And it is well for us to feel this." Martin Heidegger, "Remembrance of the Poet," in *Existence and Being*, ed. Werner Brock, trans. Douglas Scott (Chicago: Gateway, 1968), 234–35. —*Trans.*

2. I would like to note that I changed the meaning of Heidegger's text a little. For him, it seems that all commentary is a disturbance that is discord. [Heidegger: "Poems are like a bell that hangs in the open air and is already becoming out of tune through a light fall of snow that is covering it" (op. cit., 234). Heidegger borrows this image from Hölderlin's poem "Entwurf zu Kolomb," on which he comments. —*Trans.*]

3. See Friedrich Hölderlin, "Brod und Wein" ("Bread and Wine"), § 7.—*Trans.*

Sade's Reason

1. See D. A. F. de Sade, *Justine, or Good Conduct Well Chastised* (1791)

in Sade, *Justine, Philosophy in the Bedroom, and Other Writings,* ed. and trans. Richard Seaver and Austryn Wainhouse (New York: Grove Press, 1965), and D. A. F. de Sade, *Juliette* (1797), trans. Austryn Wainhouse (New York: Grove Press, 1968).—*Trans.*

2. See Jean Paulhan, "The Marquis de Sade and His Accomplice," in Sade, *Justine, Philosophy in the Bedroom, and Other Writings,* op. cit., pgs. 3–36.—*Trans.*

3. D. A. F. de Sade, *The 120 Days of Sodom* (1785), in Sade, *The 120 Days of Sodom and Other Writings,* ed. and trans. Austryn Wainhouse and Richard Seaver (New York: Grove Press, 1966).—*Trans.*

4. Pierre Klossowski, *Sade My Neighbour* (1947, 1967), trans. Alphonso Lingis (Chicago: Northwestern University Press, 1991).

5. See Maurice Heine, "Introduction," in Marquis de Sade, *Dialogue between a Priest and a Dying Man,* trans. Samuel Putnam (Chicago: P. Covici, 1927).

6. Sade has no trouble recognizing this: "Man, due to his singular tastes, is sick."

The Experience of Lautréamont

1. Rhadamanthys, son of Zeus and Europa, brother of Minos and Sarpedon, was, like his brothers, adopted by the Cretan King Asterion, to whom Zeus had given Europa. Famous for his wisdom and sense of justice, as well as his powers of judgment in meting out punishment, tradition holds that the laws Rhadamanthys delivered to the Cretans from Zeus's cave every nine years were so sure and true that, after his own death, Rhadamanthys became one of the judges of the dead in the Underworld.—*Trans.*

2. Comte de Lautréamont, *Oeuvres complètes,* introduction by Roger Caillois (Paris: Librairie José Corti, 1946). Throughout this essay, citations from *Maldoror* follow the pagination of the text of *Les Chants de Maldoror* included in [*Maldoror and the Complete Works of the Comte de Lautréamont,* trans. Alexis Lykiard (Cambridge: Exact Change, 1994)]. It will be necessary for us to designate certain stanzas by number. If one neglects the division into *Cantos, Maldoror* is composed of a total of sixty stanzas. Naturally, this convenience should not be compared with the original edition. At the same time, it seems that after the third stanza of the sixth *Canto* (stanza LIII), Lautréamont numbered each stanza from one to eight, after the fashion of chapters in a novel, Mervyn's novel, the final sections of his work, while continuing to divide them into stanzas. But to what extent did the edition of 1869–74 reproduce,

without error, the typographical details of the original manuscript? L. Genonceaux affirms that the reprint that he presented in 1890 had been reviewed and corrected based on the manuscript. This is possible, but doubtful.

3. Here and below, Blanchot refers to *The Book of Revelation* by the title *Apocalypse*. The term "apocalypse" designates the genre of *The Book of Revelation* and other first-person narratives that relate revelatory visions about the future or about life in heaven or both. *The Book of Daniel* represents another "apocalypse" in this technical sense. In what follows, we use the title *The Book of Revelation* or the term *Revelation* when referencing this work. Occasionally, Blanchot uses the word "apocalypse" in a more general sense. In such cases, we have followed his usage.— *Trans.*

4. Letter to the editor. [Auguste Poulet-Malassis, 23 October 1969. Here Blanchot follows the scholarship of his day in erroneously attributing this quotation to a letter from Lautréamont to an editor at the firm of Verboeckhoven et Cie. Mickiewicz refers to the Polish poet, dramatist, and mystic Adam Mickiewicz (1798–1855). See *Maldoror*, 258, 327, n9.—Trans.]

5. Hans Rudolf Linder, *Lautréamont: Sein Werk und sein Weltbild* (Affoltern am Albis, Buchdr: J. Weiss, 1947).

6. Notably, 208 ff.

7. Canto V, stanza from the funeral procession where Maldoror, carried by the "famous white horse," is designated as the Horseman of the Apocalypse.

8. For example, canto II, on lice: "O louse . . . as long as humanity rends its own flanks in deadly wars; as long as divine justice casts down its vengeful bolts upon this selfish globe; as long as man disregards his Creator and (not without reason) flouts him, doing so with some contempt—your reign over the universe will be assured, and your dynasty extend its links from age to age" (80–81).

9. See *Revelation* 17:1–6.— *Trans.*

10. At the beginning of this battle, the dragon says to the eagle (who is Maldoror): "I was waiting for you, and you me. The time has come; so here I am. Read, on my forehead, my name written in hieroglyphic signs" (117). But eventually this name is revealed to us—it is *Hope*—so that the eagle, defeating the dragon, triumphs over hope. As much as *Revelation*, this text reminds us of all the poems wherein Baudelaire personified Hope:

> . . . Hope
> Defeated, cries, and atrocious, despotic Agony
> on my inclined head plants his black flag.
>   —"Spleen"

> . . . Mournful spirit, yesteryear in love with the struggle,
> Hope, of which the spur stirs up your passion,
> No longer wants to straddle you! Lie down indecently,
> Old horse.
>   —"The Taste for Nothingness"

11. "Millions of enemies come crashing down in this way, on every city, like clouds of locusts," Lautréamont says over the course of that stanza (82). The strange "subterranean mine," from which the lice spill in infinite streams, would recall the "Pits of Hell," from which, like "the smoke of great furnaces," rise the storm clouds of locusts. Let's remark that St. John gives way to the same outrageousness as Lautréamont, when, describing the locusts on a large scale, he shows them as similar to jousting horses with crowns of gold on their heads, faces like the faces of man, hair like that of a woman, teeth like those of a lion (Rev 9:7–12). The lice in Maldoror are likewise infinitely small and infinitely large. The stanza concludes with the invocation, in a powerful apocalyptic tone: "Were the earth covered with lice like grains of sand on the seashore, the human race would be annihilated, stricken with terrible grief. What a spectacle! And I, with angel's wings, motionless in the sky, contemplating it!" (83).

12. Our italics. One recalls that in canto III, God, drunk with wine, stretched out on a road, is shown "*fermenting* the impure liquor" (119).

13. Mervyn writes to Maldoror, "the shadow of your love implicates a smile that, perhaps, does not exist: it is so vague, and is moving its scales so torturously!" (202).

14. Mythologists have often pointed out the fascination that the image of the snake exerts on God himself. Quintin Matsys's "Saint John at the Chalice" depicts the apostle blessing a chalice from which a dragon escaped. And the Ophite sect honored the snake as the incarnation of Wisdom and the true Christ.

15. See the *Bhagavad-Gita*: "As I watch Your terrible mouths with their various, destructive defenses, Your faces that are like the fires of Death and of Time, I lose sight of directions and I do not find peace ... All of you, with your multitude of gods and heroes ... , rush toward the terrible armed gullet of defensives, and we see, as a result of this move-

ment, heads crushed and bloodied, caught between Your powerful fangs." [The Eleventh Teaching, "The Vision of Krishna's Totality," lines 20–30.— *Trans.*]

16. Both of these lines refer us once again to the stanza cited above— "It was one spring day ..."—when the engorged and unconscious Creator sadly slept off his wine by the side of the road.

17. André Breton did not need to analyze the texts to ask for proof of their references in order to "situate" *Maldoror* in the light of Revelation: "The *definitive Apocalypse* that this work ... " (Breton's emphasis). [Breton, *Anthology of Black Humour*, trans. Mark Polizzotti (San Franscico: City Lights Books, 1997) 132–34.—Trans.]

18. See these lines from the text: "I laugh heartily to think you reproach me with spreading bitter accusations against humanity, of which I am a member (this remark alone would prove me right!)" (190).

19. See canto IV, pages 142–44.

20. Marthe Robert's translation from her *Introduction à la lecture de Kafka* (Paris: Éditions du Sagittaire, 1946).

21. "Yet I vaguely recall having given you permission to let your legs swarm over my blossoming breast" (181). A final effort to save the will of initiative, but, in the end, this last will is lost in the immensity of an irrevocable decree: "The vague promise you spoke of was not made to us but to the Being who is stronger than you: you yourself understood that it was best to submit to this irrevocable decree" (187).

22. "I carried him to the nearest cottage, for he had fainted, and left the peasants only after leaving them my purse, to purchase comforts for the wounded man, and after I made them promise to lavish upon the unfortunate—as though on their own son—the proofs of patient understanding" (141).

23. See Georges Blin, *Le Sadisme de Baudelaire* (Paris: Corti, 1948).

24. Gaston Bachelard, *Lautréamont* (1940, 1951, 1963), trans. Robert S. Dupree (Dallas, TX: The Pegasus Foundation, "The Bachelard Translations," 1986), 2.

25. Ibid., 3.

26. Ibid., 3. [Translation modified.—*Trans.*]

27. Ibid., 2.

28. Rather close to this, it seems, is the sentiment expressed by Michel Carrouges in his book *La mystique du surhomme* (Paris: Gallimard, 1948) on Lautréamont: "In such an extreme case as that of Lautréamont, one might say that he is the demon who testifies to God's existence while also

to that of the demonic" (10). And yet even more precisely: "Even a Lautréamont would not know how to behave like a dark angel without affectation, although the demonic nature of his literary work is obvious. There is no trace in him of a pure and simple atheism—a furious phobia of theology animates the text—but how can one not see therein a profoundly discontented love?" (419). Mr. Linder, concluding his study, expresses the idea in these terms: "We think we have the right to affirm that the poet of the *Maldoror*, in spite of his nihilistic and even satanic appearance, shows himself, to the person who takes pains to penetrate deeper into his literary work, as one of the most astonishing and of the most authentic of those who search for God" (107).

29. Léon-Pierre Quint's *Le Comte de Lautréamont et Dieu* (Marseille: Cahiers du Sud, 1929) has already demonstrated how these two critical methods could be reconciled.

30. But with what time? This interrogation also endures.

31. Rémy de Gourmont, *Le Livre des masques: portraits symbolistes, gloses et documents sur les écrivains d'hier et d'aujourd'hui* (Paris: Mercure de France, 1920); reprinted in José Corti's edition of Lautréamont's *Œuvres complètes* (Paris: Corti, 1958, 1961, 1963, 1969), preceded by prefaces by various authors.

32. Roger Caillois, op. cit.

33. Julien Gracq, "Lautréamont toujours," in *Œuvres complètes* (Corti).

34. "The reader ... does not very clearly see where he is at first being led; yet this feeling of remarkable stupefaction, from which one generally seeks to shield those who spend their time reading books or booklets, I have made every effort to produce" (190).

35. "One must, besides, with good mesmeric fluid, make it somnambulistically impossible for him to move, against his nature forcing his eyes to cloud over at your own fixed stare" (214).

36. See 167 ff. and 180 ff.

37. But one must immediately add: in Rimbaud, by other means, poetry is experience itself.

38. See the end of canto IV (156–58).

39. At the end of the first canto, Ducasse seems to allude to publication: "This first canto ends here ... As for me, I shall resume work to produce a second canto in not too long a time" (57).

40. We note one of them. At the beginning of stanza VI, the text from the definitive edition reads, "Oh! How sweet to snatch brutally from his bed a boy who has as yet nothing upon his upper lip, and, with

eyes open wide, to feign to stroke his forehead softly, brushing back his beautiful locks!" (31), and the text from the first printing reads, "Ah! How sweet it is to go to bed with a child who has as yet nothing on his upper lip, and to softly stroke his forehead, brushing back his beautiful locks!"

41. Nevertheless, Ducasse, also in this canto, alludes to his origins twice. In the stanza about prostitution: "It is not the spirit of God passing, only the piercing sigh of Prostitution united with the heavy groans of the Montevidean" (34). And in the last stanza: "The end of the nineteenth century shall see its poet (though at the outset he should not begin with a masterpiece, but follow the law of nature). He was born on South American shores, at the mouth of the River Plate, where two peoples once enemies now struggle to outdo each other in material and moral progress. Buenos Aires, queen of the south, and Montevideo, the coquette, extend friendly hands across the Argentine waters of the great estuary" (57).

42. In this canto, the "beautiful as" figures are imposed in their insolent splendor.

43. See Johann Wolfgang von Goethe, "Erlkönig" (c. 1782) in Goethe, *Selected Poems*, ed. Christopher Middleton (Boston: Suhfkamp/Insel Publishers, 1983), 87.—*Trans.*

44. "*Maldoror.*—Dazet, you rightfully said once: I didn't love you ..." ... "*Dazet.*—Hear me, Maldoror ... One day you called me the mainstay of your life. Since then I have not belied the trust you placed in me ... I came to snatch you from the abyss. Those who call themselves your friends, smitten with consternation, stare at you whenever they meet your pale and stooping figure ... Abandon these thoughts, which make your heart empty as a desert ... Your mind is so sick that you do not realize it, and think yourself normal every time crazy words ... gush from your mouth. Wretch!" [Compare 55–57.—*Trans.*]

45. Marcel Jean and Arpad Mezei, *Maldoror* (Paris: Éditions du Pavois, 1947), 61.

46. Always perfectly lucid, Ducasse, at the end of canto I, recognizes: "The end of the nineteenth century shall see its poet (though at the outset he should not begin with a masterpiece, but follow the law of nature)" (57).

47. "I write this on my deathbed" (43).

48. The poems of *Gaspard de la Nuit* were written by Aloysius Bertrand, then famously set to music by Maurice Ravel in 1909. Félicité-

Robert de Lamennais's *Paroles d'un Croyant: Divers Écrits pour le Peuple* (1834) is a classic of Christian Socialism, written with a lyrical intensity, rigorous logic, and mystical fervor that raises its polemic above mere pamphleteering.—*Trans.*

49. Stanza V (pages 30–31)—"I have seen"—a curiously driven stanza. The eloquence is herein almost deprived of irony, the emotion real. What has Lautréamont "seen"? Regardless of whether, in the name of glory, a will finds fulfillment in man, leading man to degradation, to perversion, or, again, if men are either openly rebelling against the heavens, or frightened by their own blasphemies, which they quiet (though, in their depths, forever hostile to the truth from on high), or, finally, if the universe, now rebelling against man, oppresses him and crushes him.

50. "Seeing these exhibitions I've longed to laugh, with the rest, but that strange imitation was impossible. Taking a penknife with a sharp-edged blade, I slit the flesh at the points joining the lips ... " (30).

51. In the fifth canto of Dante's *Inferno* we find, and in the same way, this double comparison: "As the cold makes the starling take an *irregular* flight, as this torment carries away, strikes, rejects, and brings back the guilty souls, who have no hope of having any courage returned to them. Likewise these cranes arranged along lines glide through the air and strike it with their lugubrious cries, as the shadows lifted by the storm emit silent groaning" (lines 40–49). An excerpt taken from Artaud de Montor's translation, which Ducasse surely had under his eyes.

52. This motivation may appear naïve; it will however play a very active role in Maldoror's deepest transformations. First Lautréamont says that men are not better than animals; then, better to become an animal; then, ah! to become an animal is to escape human baseness, therefore let us become swine. All this we can affirm on common grounds, which is not a pretext, but a translation, on a theoretical level, of a much deeper uneasiness, the moral alibi of true "becoming."

53. An image of Kabbalistic origin.

54. "Extend your livid claws, tearing out a pathway in your own breast ... that's it ... Oh! When you advance, crest high and fearsome, surrounded by tortuous coils as by a royal court, mesmeric and savage, rolling your waves one on the other, conscious of what you are ... " (42).

55. See the letter dated October 27, 1869, to Poulet-Malassis: "Ernest Naville (correspondent for the Institut de France), quoting philosophers and *poètes maudits*, last year gave lectures on *The Problem of Evil* at

Geneva and Lausanne that have left their mark on people's minds through an imperceptible current, which goes on expanding. He has since collected them into a single volume. I shall send him a copy. In the later impressions he will be able to mention me, for I take up with more vigor than my predecessors this strange thesis ... " (259).

56. Op. cit., 127 ff.

57. "I thank you, O rhinolophus, you whose snout is topped by a horseshoe-shaped crest, for having woken me with the motion of your wings. Indeed, I perceive it was unfortunately but a fleeting sickness, and with disgust I feel myself restored to life. Some say you approached me to suck what little blood is to be found in my body ... " (44). This image of blood had been sketched in the preceding development wherein Maldoror's nocturnal, cadaverous flight crossed "the blood-stained space": "(A rain of blood falls from my vast body, akin to the blackish cloud that the hurricane thrusts ahead.)" (44).

58. Throughout canto II, this linguistic inertia, this refusal to speak, deepens, becoming a refusal to hear: "They say that I was born in the arms of deafness!" (76). And likewise, here, paralysis surrenders, the shackles are broken, when our hero, placed in the presence of the Creator, stands up against the infamy of this spectacle: "The trammels in my ears came loose abruptly, the eardrums cracked ... " (77).

59. "So then, vile Eternal God, in viper's shape, not content with having set my soul on the frontiers of madness and those frenzied thoughts that kill slowly, you had besides, after a close survey, to deem it befitting your majesty to make a goblet of blood gush from my brow!" (61–62).

60. *Märchen* means fairy tale or story, here referring to Ducasse's imitation of Goethe's ballad. The theoretical contours and purposes of this genre were favored topics of German Romantic writers, notably Novalis.—*Trans.*

61. The stanza about the gravedigger (49–55).

62. In an equally illegitimate manner, the same violent thought comes to light in the stanza about the ocean: "Besides, from the spectacle of your fecund breasts emerges the notion of ingratitude, for one thinks immediately of those innumerable parents ungrateful enough toward the Creator to abandon the fruit of their sorry unions" (39).

63. Perhaps reminiscent of Kabbalistic or hermetic origins: "He is generally taken for a madman. One day four masked men, upon orders received, threw themselves upon him and bound him hand and foot, so

that he could move only his legs. The whip's harsh lash slashed at his back, and they told him to be on his way without delay—along the road that leads to bedlam. He began to smile while scourged and spoke to them with such feeling, such intelligence, concerning so many human sciences he had studied—displaying vast erudition for one who had not yet crossed the threshold of youth. And his discourse on humanity's destiny, during which he laid absolutely bare the poetic nobility of his soul ... " (73).

64. "O stern mathematics ... I instinctively aspired to drink from your spring, more ancient than the sun, and, most faithful of your initiates, still I continue to tread the sacred court of your grave temple. There was a haze in my spirit, something indefinable, smoky-thick, but I knew how to cross—religiously—the steps that lead to your altar, and as wind drives off the fritillary" (83).

65. "The vision of that fiery comet shall shine no more—like a sorry subject of zealous curiosity—across the façade of your disappointed observation ... " (67–68).

66. "These tresses are sacred: the hermaphrodite himself wished it. He does not want human lips piously kissing hair scented by the mountain breeze, nor his brow, aglow now like the stars of the firmament. But it is better to believe that while traversing space a star itself has descended out of orbit on to this majestic brow, and encircles it with a diamond's brilliance as a halo" (74).

67. "Sometimes, the peasant dreamer catches sight of a meteorite slicing straight through space, moving from one side low in the sky toward a corn field ... You now have, clearly and succinctly, the explanation of the phenomena."

68. See the stanza about the red lamp, in canto III (121–30) and the stanza about the hanged man, in canto IV (137–42).

69. The stanza about Falmer, canto IV, stanza XLIII (156–58).

70. The coupling must last three nights: "I tore a female louse from the hair of humanity. I was seen in bed with her for three consecutive nights, and then I cast her into the pit" (81).

71. "Standing on the rock while the hurricane lashed at my hair and cloak, I ecstatically watched the full force of the storm ... " (97–98). "It seemed to me that my hatred and my words, overcoming the distance, destroyed the physical laws of acoustics" (96).

72. "The long, chaste, and hideous coupling." Regardless of whether the memory of virginity has come to haunt what is apparently the most

contrary act to him, this is not only felt in this expression (very close to the "filthy virginity" of lice), but in the words that precede it: "Having gone three meters without exerting much effort, they (the female shark and Maldoror) fall abruptly against one another, like two lovers, and kiss with dignity and gratitude, in an embrace as that between a brother and sister. Carnal desires follow soon after the display of friendship" (99).

73. He will say at the beginning of canto III: "Leman! ... Lohengrin! ... Lombano! ... Holzer! ... for one instant, covered again with the insignia of youth, you appeared on my charmed horizon. But I let you fall back like diving-bells into chaos. You shall leave it never more" (107).

74. "Maldoror ... raises the young man without hesitation, and helps his body reject all the water. At the thought that this inert body could live again with his help, he felt his heart leap, with this fantastic idea ... Vainglorious attempts! ... The body remains inert, and lets itself be turned in all directions. He rubs its temples; he massages this and that limb; he blows for an hour into the mouth, pressing his lips against the lips of this stranger" (100).

75. The drowned of the Seine, Holzer, wanted to kill himself. This is an allusion to a fear of suicide obsessive enough for Lautréamont to have sought to protect himself from it by linking himself to it with a "promise": "O Holzer, you who thought yourself so rational and so strong, have you not seen by your very own example how hard it is in a fit of despair to keep the cool head of which you boast? I hope you will never again cause me such sorrow, and I for my part promise you never to attempt my life" (101). The same allusion appears, at the beginning of canto III: "I received life like a wound, and I have forbidden suicide to heal the scar" (112).

76. In French, *conscience* refers to both our consciousness and our conscience. This double meaning should be kept in mind throughout the following passage.—*Trans.*

77. The conscience that Maldoror pursues and that pursues him is not only moral conscience, but conscience in its most extended meaning; it is essentially fire, light, livid flame: "Light appears, with its cortege of beams, like a flight of curlew that swoops down on lavender, and man finds himself facing himself, eyes open and ashen" (102). If it "tracks man down especially in obscurity," obscurity too enters into this light: it is initially the clarity of night.

78. See canto II, in the stanza about Lohengrin (63).

79. There is however a feeling of anxiety, of vertigo, in the lines that end canto III: " ... making some brief speculations upon the dotage of the Creator who, alas!, would be causing humanity to suffer for a long time to come (eternity is long), either through cruelties inflicted or through the vile spectacle of the chancres spawned by a great vice. I closed my eyes like a drunken man at the thought of having such a being for an enemy ... " (130).

80. Stanza about the eccentric python (170–73).

81. "Maldoror ... undressed rapidly, like a man who knows what he is about. Naked as a stone, he flung himself upon the young girl's body and pulled up her dress to attempt her virtue ... in broad daylight! Not at all embarrassed, not he! Let us not dwell on this foul deed. His mind discontent, he dressed hurriedly" (114).

82. Alone, "the madwoman who dances past" remembers this story, but in a very impersonal way, because she embodies the narration. As for Maldoror, "he forgot this childhood memory," and when the manuscript fell under his eyes "he was no longer able to keep his wits about him and fainted;" at this moment, he also lost his name, he became "the stranger" (112–13).

83. At the end of this scene, the witness says this about "the distinguished stranger": "When he was satiated with sniffing this woman" (124). Debauchery, we see, singularly incomplete.

84. "Hitherto, I believed *I* was the Almighty—but no ... " (127).

85. " ... the nuns of the convent-brothel can sleep no more and wander about the courtyard gesticulating like automata, trampling buttercups and lilacs underfoot; they have gone mad from indignation, but not mad enough to forget what caused this disease of their brains ... " (127).

86. "He said that this young man trapped in the toils of my subtle tortures might perhaps have become a genius and solaced men on earth for misfortune's blows with admirable songs of poetry, of courage" (127). The adolescent's torments "literally assailed from head to toe," for having "acquiesced to the wishes of the distinguished stranger," recalls, naturally, the misfortunes and dark feelings of childhood, when strictness of the grown-ups and the pitiless, paternal authority reigned.

87. Everything suggests the secret, incompletely revealed character of the event to us: "I obliterated the original inscription and replaced it with this: 'It is painful as a dagger, keeping such a secret in one's heart, but I swear never to reveal what I witnessed" (130). Similarly, what happens between the adolescent and his torturer eludes narration and testi-

mony: "Not having the strength to raise myself up upon my smarting root, I could not see what they did" (124). I am not sure if I should here mention that François Ducasse, Isidore-Lucien's father, was, in Montevideo, "the hero of scandalous adventures."

88. It is in fact in this passage that Lautréamont, for the first time, looks unabashedly at poetry: "There will be in my lyrics an impressive proof of force and authority. He sings for himself alone and not for his fellow men. He does not weigh his inspiration upon human scales. Free as the storm, some day he shall run aground upon the indomitable shores of his terrible will! He fears nothing, unless it be himself" (137).

89. When Maldoror wants to get the rhinoceros "in whom the substance of the Savior has been introduced" (217), Mervyn's mother and father are brought forward to protect the pachyderm, a detail that clearly shows just what kind of natural alliance Lautréamont institutes between the powers above and below, familial powers in particular.

90. My emphasis.

91. A fear that is manifested in many forms, but in the clearest and simplest way in the beginning of the stanza about the shipwreck: "I sought a soul that might resemble mine, and I could not find it. I scanned all the crannies of the earth: my perseverance was useless. Yet I could not remain alone" (93).

92. "My feet have taken root in the soil, forming a sort of perennial vegetation—not quite plant life though no longer flesh—as far as my belly, and filled with vile parasites. My heart, however, is still beating. But how could it beat if the decay and effluvia of my carcass (I dare not say body) did not abundantly feed it?" (142). If we agree to recognize, between this living root, fed by death, and the hanged man of the previous stanza, a tacit secret agreement, the myth of the mandrake comes to mind. Similarly, the image of a sort of *Adam Kadmon*, a microcosm of the world of filth, seems to be superimposed on an allusion to Job. Finally, we recall that, in the seventh circle of (Dante's) Hell, men guilty of giving themselves over to death see themselves changed into bushes, plants, knotty trunks, and, at the end of time, their bodies, which they will not be able to reintegrate, will be hung, empty and vain, from the tree that they became. As such the image of the hanged man and that of the man transformed into wood appear to be associated with one another: "I made—of my own house—my gallows place" [Dante, *Inferno*, canto XIII, ln 151]. Should we also mention that the spirit of metamorphosis haunts both Dante's Hell and Maldoror's world? ["Adam

Kadmon" is the "primordial man," the first man of the Jewish Kabbala. He was the perfect prototype for man created by God.—*Trans.*

93. This incident would be too easy to interpret in vulgar psychoanalytical terms.

94. There is probably a connection between this mysterious incident and the tragic episode in canto II, when Maldoror, three times, offers up his head to the blade of the guillotine. Oh, well, says Lautréamont, "thrice my physical body—especially at the base of my neck—was shaken to the core" (105). And here again: "This sharp blade sunk up the neck between the shoulders of the fiesta bull, and its skeletal structure quaked, like an earthquake" (143). Additionally, we recall that after this vainglorious attack against his head, Maldoror predicted and accepted the intervention of a "sword," used against him by "some invisible cloud." From canto II to canto IV, the event deepens, is obscured and, gradually, the image of an openly confronted, willfully sought ordeal is substituted for the consciousness of a darker "evil" whose origin evades him.

95. "You want to know, do you not, how a sword comes to be set vertically down my back? I myself remember it none too clearly. Yet if I decide to treat as a memory what may be but a dream ... " (143).

96. "Anyone claiming that I do not possess the faculty of memory will not be wrong ... This is not the first time that the nightmare of temporary loss of memory took residence in my imagination when, by the inflexible laws of optics, I happen to be confronted with the failure to recognize my own reflection!" (147–48).

97. "Mesmerism and chloroform, when they take the pains to do so, sometimes know how to bring on similar lethargic catalepsies. They bear no resemblance to death: it would be an outright lie to say so" (148).

98. Thus it is clearly indicated that the dream of metamorphosis is linked to an effort to go beyond morality: "Now no more constraint. When I wanted to kill, I killed; this even happened often, and no one stopped me from doing it. Human laws followed me with their vengeance, but my conscience did not reproach me at all" (149).

99. "Earthly animals shunned me and I stayed alone in my resplendent grandeur. Great was my astonishment when, after swimming across a river ... I tried to walk upon that flowery bank. My feet were paralyzed ... It was then, amid uncanny efforts to continue on my way, that I awoke and realized I had become a man again" (149–50).

100. "Now that my memory has gone over the various phases of this

frightful flattening against the granite's belly, during which the tide twice passed without my noticing it over an irreducible mixture of dead matter and living flesh ... " (148).

101. It is necessary to also take into account that throughout the so very dark stanza about the guillotine and the struggle with his conscience in canto II, Maldoror, changed into an octopus, attempts, with his eight monstrous tentacles, to hug the monstrous body of the Creator, and applies his four hundred suction cups on him, so as to nourish himself abundantly with sacred blood. A ferocious, "viscous grip," but that is no different from Dazet's friendly embrace, when he is invited to press his mercury stomach "against my aluminum stomach." This reveals again the superhuman values Lautréamont associates with the erotic experience in either its cruel or tender form.

102. "Who speaks here of appropriation? Let everyone be assured that man, with his complex and manifold nature, is not unaware of the means of extending its frontiers still further: he lives in water, like the sea-horse; in the upper strata of the air, like the osprey; and below the earth, like the mole, the woodlouse, and the sublime earthworm" (152).

103. We already found this contrast expressed in canto II, when Maldoror described his soul as placed between the frontiers of madness "and thoughts of fury that slowly kill."

104. Two stanzas prior there is evoked "a man who remembers having lived a half century as a shark in the deep sea currents along the African coasts" (146), Maldoror's final transformation after his long, chaste, and hideous coupling with the female shark.

105. In the stanza about Lohengrin (canto II) wherein the fraternal theme is sketched out, the image of prison appears, connected with the same thoughts. Maldoror asks for prison as the punishment for the crime that he dreamed of committing against his friend: "So, Lohengrin, do what you will, act as you please, lock me up for life in a gloomy prison with scorpions for my cellmates" (64). (The same image of prison, this time associated with the obsession with hair, appears in the stanza about the mirror [145].)

106. When the wolf, passing by, sees this hair on the horizon, swaying in the wind, he takes flight, says Maldoror, with incomparable speed. One might say that the wolf—in whom is incarnated, as was the bulldog earlier, the animal force of base passions—sees this cut hair to be a threat to his power.

107. This figure, Gaston Bachelard says, evokes the unhappiness of

the student condemned to having his head shaved. "Who scalped you? If it was a human being—because you incarcerated him for twenty years in a prison—and who escaped so as to prepare a revenge worthy of his reprisals" (145). "Did I not recall that I too had been scalped, although it was only for five years (the exact length of time had escaped me) that I clapped a human being into prison in order to witness the spectacle of his sufferings because he had refused me—and rightly—a friendship not bestowed on beings like myself?" (147). [See Bachelard, op. cit., 36–37—*Trans.*]

108. With this clear consciousness of obscurity, with this strange knowledge capable of persevering in ignorance, Lautréamont, specifically in the stanza about Falmer, makes us feel an ambiguous power when he evokes the span of his wings plunging into his agonizing memory or when he insistently repeats: "I, too, am a scientist" (157).

109. "May it please heaven that the reader, emboldened, and become momentarily as fierce as what he reads ... " (27).

110. The amphibian (from the stanza about metamorphosis) was "webbed" to the end of his arms and legs (154). The transformation now reached his head.

111. "This woman whose arms and legs you trussed with strings of pearls in such wise as to make up an amorphous polyhedron ... has seen ... her limbs, buffed by the mechanical law of rotary fiction, blending into the unity of coagulation, and her body presenting ... the monotonous appearance of an entirely homogeneous whole that through the confusion of its various shattered components resembles only too well the mass of a sphere!" (165). Lautréamont's lively remark, "And there I was, believing it to be excrementitious substances. What an utter simpleton I am!" (167), is another wink at the interpreter. Two stanzas later the extensive movement, "O incomprehensible pederasts," begins (173 ff.).

112. "But do you know whether, despite the abnormal state of this woman's atoms, reduced to dough, ... she does not still exist?" (165).

113. "Oh! To behold one's intellect in a stranger's sacrilegious hands. An implacable scalpel probes its dense undergrowth. Conscience exhales a long rhonchus of curses; for her modesty's veil undergoes cruel rents ... Sink underground, O anonymous stigmata, and reappear to my haggard indignation no more" (168).

114. My italics. Later, in *Poésies*, Lautréamont will recommend "guard[ing] against purulent insomnias" (226).

115. We are now reminded of this text: "Each morning when the sun rises for others, spreading joy and wholesome warmth throughout all nature, none of my features stirs as I stare fixedly at space (full of shadows) ... As a condemned man soon to mount the scaffold flexes his muscles, reflecting on their fate, so, upright upon my straw pallet, my eyes shut, I turn my neck slowly, right to left, left to right, for whole hours on end. I do not fall stone dead" (36–37).

116. "Seated on the tumbril I am drawn toward the binary posts of the guillotine" (169). We saw, from canto I onward, the same images of the guillotine, of vertebral fixation, and of more or less willful immobility, all appearing to be linked to one another.

117. Stanza about Lohengrin (63–64).

118. Stanza about the excentric python (172).

119. "Thus does a cunning but not boastful mind employ the very means to gain its ends, which at first would seem to produce an insuperable obstacle. My intelligence forever aspires to this imposing question" (176).

120. "The priest of religions heads the procession, holding in one hand a white flag, the sign of peace, and in the other a golden device depicting the male and female privy parts, as if to indicate that these carnal members are, most of the time, all metaphor aside, very dangerous tools in the hands of those employing them, when manipulated blindly to different and conflicting ends ... To the small of the back is attached (artificially, of course) a horse's tail, thick and flowing, that sweeps dust off the ground. It means: beware of debasing ourselves by our behavior to the level of animals" (177). Certainly, one senses the affectation of hermeticism and the allusion to mythic memories, no less than in this passage (in the stanza about the incomprehensible pederasts): "Do you possess a sixth sense lacking in us? ... This is not an inquiry I address to you; for since I as observer see a good deal of the sublimity of your grandiose intelligences, I know where I stand. Be blessed by my left hand, be hallowed by my right, angels protected by my universal love" (173).

121. We are also reminded that, in the first version, at the end of the first canto, Dazet, mysteriously making Maldoror responsible for his death, shows him his funeral procession, of which we might be able to recognize a distant image here.

122. "And when I summarily reflect upon those sinister mysteries by which a human being disappears from the earth as easily as a fly or drag-

onfly, retaining no hope of return, I find myself nursing keen regret at probably not being able to live long enough to explain properly to you what I do not myself pretend to know. But since it has been proved that by an extraordinary chance I have not lost my life since that far-off time when, filled with terror, I began the preceding sentence, I mentally calculate that it will not be useless here to construct the complete avowal of my basic impotence ... " (178).

123. Again it is worthy to note, at the beginning of canto III, another allusion to this very fixation: "I discern in your eyes' depths a vat full of blood, in which your innocence boils—its neck bitten by the large species of scorpion" (111).

124. Here amateurs in symbolic mythology have a source of delight. Jung reminds us that, among the original powers, the one that is both male and female, when it is invoked only in its feminine side, is called Nit, mother of mothers, beetle, vulture. Now, in the stanza about the man with the pelican head, the beetle has his double in the sky, the justifiable lamb-eating vulture. It is also well known that "the terrible mother," the mother of sorcery and magicians, appears in the shape of a bladder bursting with blood, and plays the role of vampire and changes beings to her liking.

125. "The blood mixes with the water, and the water with the blood." And this too: "But then what mystery had taken place beneath the water, for a long trail of blood to be visible through the waves?" (183).

126. My emphasis of the word "parentage."

127. Maldoror's crimes are nearly always carried out in two ways: sometimes, with this "steel blade that never leaves him," the sharp-edged blade, that, in the scene of the attack of the bulldog, becomes a "steel Hydra," "American pocketknife, comprised of ten to twelve blades," a "sword," thus bringing, as compensation for the memory of failure, the option of multiple capabilities; and sometimes the aggression takes the form of a whirlwind, of a hurricane (the crime against Falmer; the dreamed crime against the young ten-year-old girl ["I could, lifting your virgin body with an iron hand, gripping you with my legs, making you roll around me like a sling, focusing my strength on describing this last circumference, and hurling you against the wall"], the crime against Mervyn). The combat of the enormous eagle (Maldoror) against the dragon already reunites the movements and images of these two forms of aggression: the eagle's flight, the "circles, of which the concentricity is growing smaller," that he draws in the air, make him into a turbulent

powerful force, but his beak, which he then plunges "in through the dragon's stomach, up to the base of his neck," a significant image, transforms him into a ferocious living blade.

128. See the passage already cited: "He and I swore eternal friendship; but one certainly different from those first two in which you had been the chief actor!" This new friendship therefore evades the drawbacks of Maldoror's flights of fancy.

129. See Bachelard, op. cit., 1. "I wish to define the astonishing unity and the overwhelming energy with which things meet in time and throughout *Maldoror*... In Lautréamont the word finds action immediately. Some poets devour or assimilate space; ... others, far fewer in number, devour time. Lautréamont is one of the greatest devourers of time, and that, as I shall show, is the secret of his insatiable violence."—*Trans.*

130. For Schopenhauer's thought on laughter, see Arnold Schopenhauer, *The World as Will and Representation*, 2 vols. Trans. E. F. J. Payne (New York: Dover Publications, 1989), 280.—*Trans.*

131. For example, "Now in this spot that my pen (this real crony who serves me as accomplice) has just made mysterious" (193). Or even, "It would show very little command of one's profession as sensational writer" (194). On Maldoror: "He scales the railing with agility and fouls the iron spikes a moment" (197).

132. Mervyn, in his sack, is mistreated less than Géronte by Scapin.

133. "I became aware I had only one eye in the middle of my forehead! O mirrors of silver, inlaid in the panels of lobbies, what services have you not rendered me by your reflective power! Since the day an Angora cat, springing suddenly onto my back, for an hour gnawed at my parietal bump like a trepan perforating the cranium" (203). Cf. canto IV, the stanza about the mirror, in which Maldoror addresses himself while not recognizing himself: "Those eyes do not belong to you ... Where did you get them? One day I saw a fair-haired woman pass before me; she had eyes like yours: you tore them from her. I see that you would lead people to believe you beautiful; but no one is fooled" (144).

134. "[T]aking the chamber-pot from under the bed puts it on Aghone's head. 'I crown you king of intellects,' he (Maldoror) exclaims with premeditated emphasis ... At night you will return the alabaster crown to its usual place, with permission to make use of it; but during the day, as soon as dawn illumines the cities, replace it on your brow as the symbol of your sway. The three Marguerites shall live again in me, not to mention that I'll be your mother" (208).

135. See canto IV: "Since I pretend to be unaware that my stare can

deal death, even to planets spinning in space" (147).

136. "He wakes as he has been ordered ... He does not try to fall asleep again ... He opens the outside shutters. He leans on the window-sill ... He waits for morning's half-light to bring, by a scene change, an absurd relief to his upset heart" (187).

137. "If death arrests the fantastic skinniness of my shoulders' two long arms—employed in the lugubrious pounding of my literary gyp-sum—I want the mourning reader at least to be able to say to himself: 'One must give him his due. He has considerably cretinised me. What wouldn't he have done had he lived longer? He's the best professor of hypnotism I ever knew!' These few touching words will be engraved on my marble tombstone, and my *manes* will be content!" (214).

138. "Pensées," recalling the *Pensées* of Blaise Pascal, so many of which Ducasse plagiarizes and modifies in his *Poésies.—Trans.*

139. Later, irony becomes "the metaphysical Gongorism of the self-parodists of my mock-heroic times" (238).

140. Words emphasized here by Lautréamont.

141. See 230–31. *The Blacksmith's Strike* (1869) is a poem by François Coppée (1842–1908), *Jocelyn* (1836) a narrative poem by the French romantic poet Lamartine (1790–1869).—*Trans.*

142. See 225.—*Trans.*

143. "If Cleopatra had been less short on morals, the face of the world would have changed. Her nose would have grown no longer" (236). See Pascal, "If Cleopatra's nose had been shorter, the face of the world would have changed."—*Trans.*

144. "A banal truth contains more genius than the works of Dickens, Gustave Aymard, Victor Hugo, Landelle" (240).

145. "The science that I undertake is distinct from poetry. I do not sing about the latter. I force myself to discover its source" (246). "A logic exists for poetry" (245). "There is the stuff of poetry in the moralists, the philosophers. Poets contain the thinker" (246). "Judgments of poetry have more value than the poetry. It is the philosophy of poetry. Philosophy, thus comprised, encompasses poetry" (242). "A philosophy for the sciences exists. There is not one for poetry ... This is odd, some might say" (244). "The writer, without singling out one in particular, can indicate the law that governs each of his poems" (242). "The phe-nomenon passes. I seek laws" (242).

146. "The theorem is mockery by nature. It is not indecent" (246).

147. "Poetry must be made by all. Not by one. Poor Hugo! Poor

Racine! Poor Coppée! Poor Corneille! Poor Boileau! Poor Scarron! Tics, tics, and tics" (244). "The existence of tics having been established, let none be surprised to see the same words recur more than their fair share: in Lamartine, the tears that fall down his horse's nostrils, the color of his mother's hair; in Hugo, the darkness and the broken man; these are part of the binding" (246). "Whatever a man's intelligence may be, the process of thought must be the same for all" (246).

Crossing Aesthetics